First World War
and Army of Occupation
War Diary
France, Belgium and Germany

21 DIVISION
63 Infantry Brigade
York and Lancaster Regiment
10th (Service) Battalion
10 September 1915 - 1 August 1916

WO95/2158/4

The Naval & Military Press Ltd
www.nmarchive.com
Published in association with The National Archives

Published by

The Naval & Military Press Ltd

Unit 10 Ridgewood Industrial Park,

Uckfield, East Sussex,

TN22 5QE England

Tel: +44 (0) 1825 749494

www.naval-military-press.com

www.nmarchive.com

This diary has been reprinted in facsimile from the original. Any imperfections are inevitably reproduced and the quality may fall short of modern type and cartographic standards.

© Crown Copyright

Images reproduced by permission of The National Archives, London, England, 2015.

Contents

Document type	Place/Title	Date From	Date To
Heading	WO95/2158/4		
Heading	21st Division 63rd Infy Bde 10th Bn York & Lancs Regt Sep 1915-Jly 1916 To 37 Div 63 Bde		
Heading	63rd Inf. Bde. 21st Div. Battn. disembarked Boulogne from England 11.9.15 War Diary September 10.9.15-29.9.15 1915 Attached: Appendices I & II.		
War Diary	Folkstone	10/09/1915	10/09/1915
War Diary	Boulogne	11/09/1915	11/09/1915
War Diary	Pont, A Briques	11/09/1915	11/09/1915
War Diary	Watten	11/09/1915	11/09/1915
War Diary	Nortebecourt	12/09/1915	20/09/1915
War Diary	Campagne	21/09/1915	21/09/1915
War Diary	St Hilaire	22/09/1915	22/09/1915
War Diary	Auchel	22/09/1915	24/09/1915
War Diary	Sailly La Bourse	25/09/1915	25/09/1915
War Diary	Vermelles	25/09/1915	25/09/1915
War Diary	Noyelles Les Vermelles	27/09/1915	28/09/1915
War Diary	Rely	29/09/1915	29/09/1915
Heading	Appendices I & II		
Miscellaneous	Report Of Operation 25th-26th Sept 1915 by 10th York & Lancs Regt Appendix I		
Miscellaneous	10th (S) Battn York & Lancs Regt Appendix II		
Heading	21st Division 10th York & Lancaster Vol 2 Oct 15		
Heading	War Diary of 10th (S) Battn York & Lancaster Regt From 2 October 1915 to 31st October 1915 Volume II		
War Diary	Rely	01/10/1915	01/10/1915
War Diary	Thiennes	01/10/1915	02/10/1915
War Diary	Borre	02/10/1915	15/10/1915
War Diary	Strazeele	15/10/1915	24/10/1915
War Diary	Steenwerke	24/10/1915	26/10/1915
War Diary	Armentieres	26/10/1915	27/10/1915
Miscellaneous	63rd Inf Brigade. Division Corps Appendix I		
Miscellaneous	10th (S) Battn York & Lancs Regt Roll of Offices Joining Appendix II	31/10/1915	31/10/1915
Miscellaneous	10th (Service) Bn York & Lancs Regt Roll of Casualties Appendix III	31/10/1915	31/10/1915
Heading	21st Division 10th York & Lancs Vol 3 Nov 15 121/7656		
Heading	War Diary of (S) Battn York & Lancaster Regt From 1st November to 29th November 1915 (Volume III)		
War Diary	Armentieres	01/11/1915	29/11/1915
Miscellaneous	10th (S) Battn York & Lancs Regt Roll Officers Joining. Appendix I	29/11/1915	29/11/1915
Miscellaneous	10th (S) Bn York & Lancs Regiment Roll Of Casualties Appendix II	29/11/1915	29/11/1915
Heading	21st Div 10th York & Lancs Vol 4 December 1915 121/7910		
Heading	War Diary of 10th (S) Battn York & Lancaster Regiment From 30th November 1915 to 1st January 1916 (Volume IV)		

War Diary	Armentieres	30/11/1915	01/01/1916
War Diary	Armentieres	02/12/1915	02/12/1915
Miscellaneous	10th (S) Bn. York & Lancs Regt Reinforcement joining Battalion during month of December 15 Appendix I		
Miscellaneous	10th (S) Bn. York & Lancs Regt Roll of Casualties during month of December 1915 Appendix II	26/12/1915	26/12/1915
Heading	21st 10th York & Lancs Vol. 5		
Heading	War Diary of 10th (S) Battn. York & Lancaster Regt. From 2nd January 1916 to 4th Febry. 1916 Volume V		
War Diary	Armentieres	02/01/1916	04/02/1916
Miscellaneous	10th (S) Bn York & Lancs Regt Reinforcements. (Appendix I)		
Miscellaneous	10th (S) Bn York & Lancs Regt Casualties. (Appendix II)	06/02/1916	06/02/1916
Heading	War Diary of 10th (S) Battn York & Lanc Regt From 4th Febry 1916 to 29th Febry 1916 Volume VI		
War Diary	Armentieres	04/02/1916	26/02/1916
Miscellaneous	10th (S) Bn. York & Lancs Regt. Reinforcements during February 1916 App I	01/03/1916	01/03/1916
Miscellaneous	10th (S) Bn. York & Lancs Regt. Casualties during February 1916 App. II	01/03/1916	01/03/1916
Heading	War Diary Of The 10th (S) Battn York & Lancaster Regt 1st Of March 1916 to 1st of April 1916 Volume VII		
War Diary	Armentieres	01/03/1916	17/03/1916
War Diary	La Creche	20/03/1916	20/03/1916
War Diary	Strazeele	21/03/1916	25/03/1916
War Diary	Allonville	01/04/1916	01/04/1916
Miscellaneous	10th (S) Battn. York & Lancaster Regt. Reinforcements joining Battn during March 1916 App I		
Miscellaneous	10th (S) Battn. York & Lancaster Regt Casualties incurred during March 1916 App II		
Heading	10th (S) Battn York & Lancaster Regt War Diary From 1st April 1916 to 30th April 1916 Volume VIII		
War Diary	Allonville	02/04/1916	02/04/1916
War Diary	Buire and Ancre	03/04/1916	03/04/1916
War Diary	Meaulte	04/04/1916	08/04/1916
War Diary	Buire and Ancre	09/04/1916	14/04/1916
War Diary	Meaulte	15/04/1916	15/04/1916
War Diary	La Neaville	22/04/1916	28/04/1916
Miscellaneous	10th (Service) Bn. York & Lancaster Regt. Appendix I		
Miscellaneous	10th (Service) Bn. York & Lancaster Regt. Appendix II		
Heading	10th (S) Battn York & Lancs Regt War Diary From 1st May 1916 to 30th May 1916 Volume IX		
Miscellaneous	Officer i/c New Army Infy Section No. 2	03/06/1916	03/06/1916
War Diary	La Neuville	01/05/1916	01/05/1916
War Diary	Bray Sur Somme	02/05/1916	02/05/1916
War Diary	Meaulte	12/05/1916	21/05/1916
War Diary	Buire	22/05/1916	22/05/1916
War Diary	La Neuville	22/05/1916	22/05/1916
Miscellaneous	10th (Ser) Bn. York & Lancaster Regiment. Casualties incurred during May 1916 Appendix II		
Miscellaneous	10th (Ser) Bn. York & Lancaster Regiment. Reinforcements arriving during the month of May 1916 Appendix I		

Heading	War Diary of 10th Bn. York and Lancaster Regt. From 1st June 1916 to 30th June 1916 Volume X		
War Diary	La Neuville	01/06/1916	01/06/1916
War Diary	Buire	02/06/1916	07/06/1916
War Diary	Meaulte.	11/06/1916	15/06/1916
War Diary	Trenches	16/06/1916	19/06/1916
War Diary	La Neuville	20/06/1916	20/06/1916
War Diary	Ville	27/06/1916	27/06/1916
Miscellaneous	10th (Ser) Bn. York & Lancaster Regiment. Casualties incurred during the month of June 1916 Appendix		
Operation(al) Order(s)	Operation Orders By Lieut-Col. J.H. Ridgway Comdg. 10th (S) Bn. York & Lancaster Regiment. 23rd June 1916 App. I	23/06/1916	23/06/1916
Operation(al) Order(s)	Amendment No. 1 to Operations Orders. dated 23/6/16	23/06/1916	23/06/1916
Miscellaneous	Instructions as to Re-Bombardment. Appendix No 1		
Operation(al) Order(s)	Addition to Operation Order No. 1 dated 23/6/1916	29/06/1916	29/06/1916
Miscellaneous	Appendix No. 2 to Operation Orders dated 23/6/1916	24/06/1916	24/06/1916
Miscellaneous	Amendment No. 2 to Operation Orders. dated 23/6/16	24/06/1916	24/06/1916
Miscellaneous	Appendix No. 3 to Operation Orders	23/06/1916	23/06/1916
Miscellaneous	Amendment No. 2 to Operation Orders. dated 23/7/16	24/06/1916	24/06/1916
Miscellaneous	Amendment No. 4 to Operation Orders, dated 23/6/16	23/06/1916	23/06/1916
Miscellaneous	Amendment No. 5 to Operation Orders dated 23/6/16	26/06/1916	26/06/1916
Miscellaneous	Amendment No. 6 to Operation orders dated 23/6/16	28/06/1916	28/06/1916
Miscellaneous	Reference Battalion Orders, dated 23/6/1916, and Amendments.	30/06/1916	30/06/1916
Miscellaneous	Operation Orders No. 2 By Lieut-Col. J.H. Ridgway. Comdg. 10th (S) Bn. York & Lancaster Regt.	25/06/1916	25/06/1916
Miscellaneous	Reference Operation Order No. 2, dated 25/6/1916	25/06/1916	25/06/1916
Miscellaneous	Extract from 63rd Brigade Orders, dated 30th July 1916 App III	30/07/1916	30/07/1916
Heading	10th (Service) Battalion York and Lancaster Regiment. War Diary July 1918 Vol 11		
War Diary	Ville	30/06/1916	30/06/1916
War Diary	Trenches	01/07/1916	03/07/1916
War Diary	Dernancourt	04/07/1916	04/07/1916
War Diary	Vaux-En-Amienois Talmas	08/07/1916	08/07/1916
War Diary	Mondicourt	09/07/1916	09/07/1916
War Diary	Trenches	11/07/1916	11/07/1916
War Diary	Humbercamp	14/07/1916	14/07/1916
War Diary	Sars-Les-Bois	15/07/1916	15/07/1916
War Diary	Bailleul-Aux-Cornaille	16/07/1916	16/07/1916
War Diary	Estree-Cauchie	18/07/1916	20/07/1916
War Diary	Trenches	25/07/1916	28/07/1916
War Diary	Camblain L'Abbe	01/08/1916	01/08/1916
Miscellaneous	List of Appendices.		
Miscellaneous	10th (Ser) Battn. York & Lancaster Regt. Operations July 1st 1916-July 4th 1916	01/07/1916	01/07/1916
Miscellaneous	Appendix No. IV Casualties incurred during Fighting July 1st/3rd 1916		
Miscellaneous	10th (S) Bn. York & Lancaster Regiment. List of Casualties incurred during Fighting. 1/7/16-3/7/16	01/07/1916	01/07/1916
Miscellaneous	Amended Casualties		
Miscellaneous	The Following letter has been received from the G.O.C. 21st Division App V	08/07/1916	08/07/1916
Miscellaneous	Operation Orders O.C. Companies and Section App VI	12/07/1916	12/07/1916

Miscellaneous	Operations Orders By Lieut-Col. J.H. Ridgway. Comdg. 10th (S) Bn. York & Lancaster Regt. 14th July 1916 App VII	14/07/1916	14/07/1916
Miscellaneous	Operations Orders By Lieut-Col. J.H. Ridgway. Comdg. 10th (S) Bn. York & Lancaster Regiment. 14th July 1916 App VIII	14/07/1916	14/07/1916
Miscellaneous	Operations Orders By Lieut-Col. Ridgway. Comdg. 10th Battn. York & Lancaster Rgt. 15th July 1916 App IX	15/07/1916	15/07/1916
Miscellaneous	Operation Orders By Lt-Colonel J.H. Ridgway Comdg. 10th Battn. York & Lanc. Rg. 18th July 1916 App X	18/07/1916	18/07/1916
Miscellaneous	Operation Orders. By Lieut-Colonel. J.H. Ridgway Comdg. 10th (S) Bn. York & Lancaster Regiment. 25th July 1916 App XI	25/07/1916	25/07/1916
Miscellaneous	Operation Orders. By Lieut-Colonel. J.H. Ridgway Comdg. 10th (S) Bn. York & Lancaster Regiment. 30th July 1916 App XII	30/07/1916	30/07/1916
Miscellaneous	10th (Service) Battn. York & Lancaster Regiment. Casualties incurred during the month of July 1916 App XIII		
Miscellaneous	Addition to Orders for Relief.	30/07/1916	30/07/1916

100 951 2158 14

21ST DIVISION
63RD INFY BDE

10TH BN YORK & LANCS REGT
SEP 1915 – JLY 1916

To 37 DIV 63 BDE

21ST DIVISION
63RD INFY BDE

63rd Inf.Bde.
21st Div.

Battn. disembarked
Boulogne from
England 11.9.15.

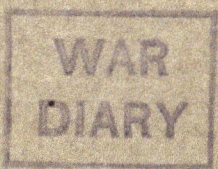

10th BATTN. THE YORK & LANCASTER REGIMENT.

S E P T E M B E R

(10.9.15-29.9.15)

1 9 1 5

Attached:

Appendices I & II.

Army Form C. 2118

WAR DIARY
or
INTELLIGENCE SUMMARY.
(Erase heading not required.)

Instructions regarding War Diaries and Intelligence Summaries are contained in F.S. Regs., Part II. and the Staff Manual respectively. Title pages will be prepared in manuscript.

Army Form C. 2118

WAR DIARY
or
INTELLIGENCE SUMMARY
(Erase heading not required.)

10/York & Lancs. Regt.

September 1915

Place	Date	Hour	Summary of Events and Information	Remarks and references to Appendices
FOLKSTONE	10/9/15	10.30pm	Left on the "Duchess of Argyll" for BOULOGNE	
BOULOGNE	11/9/15	1.30am	Arrived – proceeded to rest Camp OSTROHOVE arrived 2.30 am	
PONT A BRIQUES	11/9/15	2.30pm	Entrained for WATTEN	
WATTEN	11/9/15	11.0pm	Arrived Proceeded at once by march route to NORTBECOURT	
NORTBECOURT	12/9/15	2 am	Arrived Clear billets (Brigade training continued)	
NORTBECOURT	20/9/15	6 pm	Marched route via ST OMER	
CAMPAGNE	21/9/15	1 am	Arrived Clear billets	
CAMPAGNE	21/9/15	7.30pm	March route via AIRE	
St HILAIRE	22/9/15	12.45 am	Arrived Clear billets	
St HILAIRE	22/9/15	7 pm	March route to AUCHEL Clear billets	
AUCHEL	22/9/15	10 pm	Arrived Clear billets	
AUCHEL	24/9/15	7 pm	March route to SAILLY LA BOURSE Bivouacked for night	
SAILLY LA BOURSE	25/9/15	3 pm	March route to VERMELLES	
VERMELLES	25/9/15	10 pm	Arrived & went straight into action towards HULLUCH – LENS road and HILL 70 relieved by the Scots Guards 3.30 am 27/9/15	Appendix I attached
NOYELLES LES VERMELLES	27/9/15	7 am	Returned from action having lost approx 360 all ranks. Returns corrected 3/10/15 to 14 officers 306 O.R. Killed Wounded Missing 1 Relieving horse 1 H.B. horse to Draught mules 5 Pack mules	Returns & route there are Appendix II
NOYELLES LES VERMELLES	28/9/15	7 pm	Moved by road & rail to RÉLY via NEUX fond very heavily	
RELY	29/9/15	11 am	Arrived (Clear billets)	

APPENDICES I & II.

(Appendix 1.)

Report of Operations 25th – 26th Sept. 1915 by 10th York & Lancr Regt.

On arrival at N. Corner of Loos G 29 D 65 received orders to proceed as fast as possible to pn 64 E of LOOS – HAISNES Rd and that the Regiment would form reserve with 12th West York Regt to an attack on HULLUCH – LENS Road.

This was carried out until the leading Battalions (Lincoln and 8th Somerset Regts) had crossed the HULLUCH – LENS Road when orders to move nrde to the N and take up an entrenched position on the HULLUCH – LENS Road facing E. The line when taken up extended from RED HOUSE by CHALK PIT E of Square Wood at pt. H 25 a 4 6 to junction of roads at H 19 C 5 9.

On arrival I reported the fact to the Brigadier. Though entrenched one had to keep down as sniping was persistent from direction of Hill 70, or Square Wood.

About 8.30 a.m a verbal order came for 2 companies to attack Square Wood. B. & C. Coys. were detailed for the purpose and I took these two Coys personally. The remaining two Coys fell back on road Hulluch – Lens and as we were hard pressed in the Square Wood A. Coy was sent up to reinforce. No further orders were received from the Brigade. As the other side of the wood was reached, a very heavy machine gun fire from concealed positions drove us back. While the attack was being made D. Coy again took up the original position on the HULLUCH - LENS road with Right resting on RED HOUSE by Chalk pit, and eventually linked up with 8 Somerset L.I.

The three Coys. driven out of the square wood on M 25 a fell back on southern road LOOS - HULLUCH. Rallied at this place together with a number of the Scotch Brigade. During the attack through the wood "C" Coy. lost all Officers, the Commander Captain D.W.S.S. Abbott I regret to say was shot and died shortly after while being carried back.

After the sunken road was held for some time, it was seen that the position was untenable as guns placed in the vicinity N.E. of BENIFONTAINE raked this road & reports received were that the Germans were there in force. A Lt. Colonel in the Scotch Brigade considered that this line should move back into the Southernmost German trenches. On this retirement as no reports were received we had no means of communicating with troops on the left, the Colonel made the above decision under very heavy machine gun and gun fire. This movement was taking place when Captain Foster, Div. Staff, suggested

a rally on a line parallel to a track running
N.E. I took charge of this which consisted
of cover from this line. Other lines were
formed in rear. After the first line had passed
through this line advanced and eventually became
part of the firing line with objective square wood
in H.258. This attack met with strong opposition
from machine gun fire from concealed guns.
Another rally was made in the sunken road Southern
road LOOS - Hulluch and this was eventually
evacuated as in the preceding case. By this
time the Regiment had lost a good number of
Officers and men. This was repeated 4
times during the course of the afternoon but
was impossible for the troops to get beyond
a line drawn N.E. from second O O in
LOOS. After these four gallant attempts
were made but the machine gun fire was too
powerful and the men were in a very exhausted
condition. All ranks worked very hard to
attain the objective but could not locate the
exact position of the concealed machine guns.
After the fourth attempt it was seen that a
general retirement as far back as the German
trenches was taking place. I collected men
of the 63rd Brigade at pt G.25 and soon
put them in the Trenches N.E. of the road.
After a short period Colonel Denny
8th Somerset L.I. arrived and I handed

over Command. I regret to report that in addition to the death of Captain Abbott 13 other Officers are wounded or missing and about 400 men are unaccounted for yet.

C.J. Averist Major
Comdg 10th York & Lancaster
W Regt.

Refce. maps. 5a (Hooge area), 36 b, 36 c.

[Appendix II]

10th (S) Battn York & Lancs Regt

Roll of Casualties (Officers) during Action 25th/26th Septr. 1915.

KILLED.
- Capt. ABBOTT, D.W.S.E.
- " LOFTUS, H.G.
- Lieut SMITH, P.L.

WOUNDED.
- Capt. MITFORD, A.H.
- " HOLMES, W.G.
- " WILLIS, A.J.
- 2/Lt. MEIN, W.H.
- " MORTON SMITH, F.
- " ROBINSON, A.R.
- " SWALLOW, H.L.St.G.

WOUNDED & MISSING.
- Lieut WHITAKER, G.G.
- " GROVES, S.J.S.
- " WHITHAM, G.S.

GASSED, but recovering.
- 2/Lt. DRAKE, D.H.

121/7595

21st Kuvein

10th York Lancaster
Vol 2
Oct 15

CONFIDENTIAL.

WAR DIARY

— of —

10th (S) Battn. YORK & LANCASTER Regt.

From 2nd October 1915 to 31st October 1915.

(Volume II)

Army Form C. 2118.

WAR DIARY
or
INTELLIGENCE SUMMARY.

(Erase heading not required.)

10/York & Lancs. Regt.

October 1915

Instructions regarding War Diaries and Intelligence Summaries are contained in F. S. Regs., Part II. and the Staff Manual respectively. Title pages will be prepared in manuscript.

Place	Date	Hour	Summary of Events and Information	Remarks and references to Appendices
RELY	1/10/15	6.30 am	Marched to THIENNES via AIRE	
THIENNES	1/10/15	12 noon	arrived (clear billets)	
THIENNES	2/10/15	7.30 am	Moved route to BORRE via HAZEBROUCK	
BORRE	2/10/15	11.30 am	arrived. found clean billets.	

WAR DIARY
or
INTELLIGENCE SUMMARY

Army Form C. 2118

(Erase heading not required.)

Place	Date	Hour	Summary of Events and Information	Remarks and references to Appendices
BORRE	6.10.15	4.30pm	Draft of 48 men arrived from from the 11th Bn York Lancaster Regt	Appendix I
BORRE	7.10.15	2.30pm	Inspection by Divisional Commander and also General Plumer	Recommendation forwarded
BORRE	9.10.15	5.7pm	Draft of 100 men arrived from 3rd & 13th Lancaster Regt	63rd Bde
BORRE	11.10.15	7.7pm	13 men - Prisoners (absent when unit embarked) arrived	21st Division
BORRE	13.10.15	8.30pm	8 officers from the 11th Bn York Lancaster Regt arrived	
BORRE	15.10.15	2.0pm	March route to STRAZEELE	See Appx II
STRAZEELE	15.10.15	3.15pm	Arrived and went into billets	
STRAZEELE	15.10.15	7.15pm	Draft of 1 officer 181 other ranks arrived from Base	
STRAZEELE	16.10.15	3pm	Major Paver - 2nd in Command proceeded to ENGLAND to report to War Office	
STRAZEELE	19.10.15	8.30am	Inspection by G.O.C. 2nd Corps	
STRAZEELE	21.11.15	7.0pm	14 men from Clearing Station (wounded etc) arrived	
STRAZEELE	24.10.15	9am	March route to via BAILLEUL	
STEENWERKE	24.10.15	12.30pm	Arrived - went into Clean billets	
STEENWERKE	26.10.15	3pm	March route	
ARMENTIERES	26.10.15	6.30pm	Arrived went into Clean billets	
ARMENTIERES	27.10.15	—	Engaged in Trench work - in line of defence under C.R.E. 50th Division	Casualties Appendix III

(Appendix I)

63rd Inf Brigade.   Division.   Corps.   (Corps Register Number.)

Schedule No. To be left Blank.	Unit.	Regtl. No.	Rank & Name.	Action for which commended.	Recommended By.	Honour or Reward.	To be left Blank.
	10 Y & Lancs		Lt. Francis Barrington Baker.	When detachment on right of regiment had been driven in this officer very ably and with great coolness seconded the efforts of the Brigade Major and formed a firing line on HULLUCH LENS Road.			
	"		Major Cecil Hugh Taylor	In rallying his Company & holding on to the CHALK PIT for a considerable time.			
	"	10/17741	Pte Cuthbert Waterhouse Binns.	When Lt.P.L.Smith was wounded, on stretcher bearers refusing to carry stretcher owing to heavy shell fire Private Binns & another Private (since killed) volunteered to carry Lt.Smith in, On the Private as above being killed Pte Farimond volunteered to take his place and with Pte Binns brought Lt.Smith in across an area swept by rifle, machine gun, and shell fire.			
	"	10/13641	Pte. John Farimond				

Capt & Adjt
Frank Taylor

Showed great coolness and devotion to duty throughout the day and by his coolness and indifference to danger set a…

10th (S) Battn. York & Lancs. Regt.   Appendix II

Roll of Officers joining.

Rank & Name		Remarks
Lieut.	RAMSDEN, J.H.	} Arrived 15th Octr/15
2/Lt	WILKINSON, R.N.	
"	KNOWLES, F.E.	
"	BAINES, C.	
"	BURSTOW, E.E.	
"	COCKBURN, E.C.	
"	KINGSFORD, R.J.	
"	BRIGGS, O.	
2/Lt	PAYNE, F.E.	Arrived 16th Octr/15.

F. Taylor, Capt & Adjt
10 York & Lancs Regt

31/10/1915

(Appendix III)

10th (Service) Bn York & Lancs Regt.

Roll of Casualties.

Regtl. no.	Rank & Name.		Remarks.
10/4478	Sergt.	LEATHAM, A	} Wounded 29th Oct/15.
3/22672	Pte.	PARKINSON, J	
20643	L/Cpl.	LLOYD, J.	}
1/20128	"	MARTIN, C.	
10/12720	"	WHITEHEAD, G.	} Wounded 30th Oct/15.
10/15323	Pte	BUTTON, J.	
10/16761	"	RAFTER, J.	
2820	"	ROWLANDS, W.	

F Naylor Capt & Adjt
10th York & Lanc. Regt

31/10/1915

10th York Lanc:
Vol: 3

121/7656

31st K'itwiin

Nov 15.

CONFIDENTIAL.

WAR DIARY

— of —

10th (S) Battn. York & Lancaster Regt

— o —

From 1st November — To 29th November 1915.

(Volume III)

Army Form C. 2118

WAR DIARY
or
INTELLIGENCE SUMMARY
(Erase heading not required.)

Instructions regarding War Diaries and Intelligence Summaries are contained in F.S. Regs., Part II. and the Staff Manual respectively. Title Pages will be prepared in manuscript.

Place	Date	Hour	Summary of Events and Information	Remarks and references to Appendices
ARMENTIERES	1.11.15		Two officers (one from 11th Rn York & Lanc's Regt & one from Training College ST OMER) arrived	Appendix I
ARMENTIERES	3.11.15	9.0 a.m	Battn HQ, Coy Comdrs, and Section Comdrs, Section Sgts, & Section Cmdrs of two platoons for Coy went into trenches with 150TH INF BDE for instructional purposes.	
ARMENTIERES	4.11.15	9.0 a.m	Platoon Cmdrs, Section Sgts and Section Cmdrs of remaining two platoons for Coy went into trenches for instructional purposes returning to billets morning of 5th. 4/11/15 [7.0 a.m. returning for Coy]	
ARMENTIERES	4.11.15	5.0 p.m	Officers N.C.O.'s & men of two platoons per Coy went into trenches for instructional purposes returning to billets m 5th	
ARMENTIERES	5.11.15	5.0 p.m	Officers, N.C.O's & men of remaining platoons as above.	
ARMENTIERES	14.11.15	7.0 p.m	The Battalion relieved the 8TH SOM. L.I. in trenches 70, 71, 72, 73. - 8th trenches on our right 10 Yorkshires on our left - relieved m 16th by 1 Lincolns.	Appendix II (Casualties) Appendix I Appendix II (Casualties)
ARMENTIERES	17.11.15	8.0 p.m	Battalion relieved by 8TH SOM. L.I.	
ARMENTIERES	21.11.15	7.0 p.m	Battalion relieved the 8TH S.L.I. as above.	
ARMENTIERES	24.11.15	9.0 p.m	5 Officers + 12 men arrived from Rouen. 4 Officers from 11th York & Lanc's. 1 Off. from ETAPLES.	
ARMENTIERES	25.11.15	8.0 p.m	Battalion relieved by 8TH S.L.I.	
ARMENTIERES	29.11.15	7.0 p.m	Battalion relieved 8TH S.L.I. as above	

10th (S) Battn. York & Lancr Regt.

Appendix I.

Roll of Officers joining.

Rank & Name		Remarks
2/Lt.	HEALD, J.A.	From 11th Bn York & Lancr. Regt. Arrived 1st Nov't/15
"	STAINTON, R.M.	From Training Corps, St Omer, Arrived 1st Nov't/15.
"	MEIN, W.H.	Rejoined from Base, Etaples; Arrived 24th Nov't/15.
"	DE WINTON, K.L.	From 11th Bn York & Lancr. Regt. Arrived 24th Nov't/15.
"	FAIRNIE, E.G.J.	
"	AYRES, J.	
"	MITCHELL, R.J.	

Numbers of Other ranks joining

Date of Arrival	No	Remarks
24th Nov't/15	Twelve.	

29th Nov't 1915.

H.P. Bryan
Lieut & Adjt.
10th Bn York & Lancr Regt.

10th (S) Bn. York & Lancaster Regiment.   Appendix E

Roll of Casualties.

Officers.

Rank & Name	Remarks
Major TAYLOR, C.H.	18th Nov/15. Shrapnel wound. Evacuated to England.

Other ranks.

Regtl No	Rank & Name	Remarks	
10/16509	Pte FRANCE, A.	KILLED in ACTION	16/11/15
10619	" SILVESTER, T.	WOUNDED in ACTION	17/11/15
21268	" BLACKSHAW, C.F.	- do -	17/11/15
21662	" MACDONALD, T.H.	- do -	21/11/15
21444	" SOUTH, W.T.	- do -	23/11/15
10/15737	" STANDISH, W.	- do -	24/11/15
3/21666	Sgt REVILL, H.	- do -	24/11/15
10/15730	Pte SOUDET, C.	KILLED in ACTION	24/11/15

H.P. Organ
Lieut & Adjt.
10th York & Lancs Regt

29th Nov/1915.

21st KRR

10th York Rangers
Vol 4
December 1915

12/7910

CONFIDENTIAL

WAR DIARY

— of —

10th (S) Battn. York & Lancaster Regiment

From 30th November 1915 — To 1st January 1916.

(Volume IV)

Army Form C. 2118

WAR DIARY
or
INTELLIGENCE SUMMARY
(Erase heading not required.)

Instructions regarding War Diaries and Intelligence Summaries are contained in F.S. Regs., Part II. and the Staff Manual respectively. Title Pages will be prepared in manuscript.

Place	Date	Hour	Summary of Events and Information	Remarks and references to Appendices
ARMENTIERES	30/11/15	7 p.m.	Battn. relieved 8 S.L.I. in trenches 70, 71, 72 & 73 — 8th [Indian?] on our right, 10th R. John. on left.	
ARMENTIERES	3/12/15	8 p.m.	Battn. relieved by 8 S.L.I. in trenches 70, 71, 72 & 73.	App. II (Casualties)
ARMENTIERES	9/12/15	7 p.m.	Battn. relieved 8 S.L.I. as above.	
ARMENTIERES	16/12/15	3.15 a.m.	Attack on Enemies trenches by 8 S.L.I. After the attack was over the Germans heavily shelled our trenches. (Our casualties in respect of this — 3 killed, 25 wounded.)	App. II (Casualties)
ARMENTIERES	17/12/15	4 p.m.	Battn. relieved by 8 S.L.I., as above.	
ARMENTIERES	18/12/15	6.30 a.m.	The enemy blew up a couple of mines in front of Mushroom, between our own and their trenches. Caused no material damage to our lines, but created a couple of large craters which the enemy afterwards attempted to occupy. They were repulsed.	App. II (Casualties)
ARMENTIERES	21/12/15	7 p.m.	Battn. relieved ≠ 8 S.L.I., as above.	
ARMENTIERES	24/12/15	8 p.m.	Battn. relieved by 8 S.L.I., as above.	
ARMENTIERES	26/12/15	5 p.m.	One Coy. ("B") of Battn. went into trenches (Trench 70) to relieve a Coy. of 8 S.L.I.	App. II (Casualties)
ARMENTIERES	28/12/15	7 p.m.	Remaining three Coys. went into trenches to complete relief of 8 S.L.I. Three Coys. occupying the front trenches, remaining Coy. to stay in reserve.	
ARMENTIERES	1/1/16	4 p.m.	Battalion relieved by 8 S.L.I., as above.	App. II (Casualties)
ARMENTIERES	2/1/15	7 p.m.	Draft of six men arrived.	See Appendix (roll)

F Taylor Major
10th R.(S) Bn. York & Lancs. Regt.

Appendix 1

10th (S) Bn. York & Lancr. Regt.

Reinforcements joining Battalion during month of December/15.

Officers

– NIL –

Other Ranks.

2nd December — six.

F Taylor Major.
10th (S) Bn York & Lancr. Regt

Appendix II

10th (S) Bn. York & Lancr. Regt.

(1)

ROLL of CASUALTIES.
during month of December 1915.

Officers.

Rank & Name		Remarks
2/Lt.	Hall, D.A.	Wounded in Action 22/12/15
"	Brigg, O.	— ditto —
* "	Wilkinson, R.N.	— ditto —
"	Burstow, E.E.	Wounded in Action, 28/12/15

* Rejoined 26th Dec't 1915.

Other ranks.

Regtl. No.	Rank & Name		Remarks
17741	Pte.	Binns, C.W.	} Killed in Action 1st Dec't 1915.
13649	"	Swindells, J.	
17229	Pte	Cartwright, J.	} Killed in Action 16th Dec't 1915.
14056	Sgt	Barnett, W.H.	
19735	L/C.	Cartwright, A.	

Roll of Casualties.
(continued)

Regtl. No.	Rank + Name		Remarks.
3413	Pte.	Stewart, W.	} Killed in Action 23rd Dec/15.
19548	"	Cooper, J.A.	
18759	Pte.	Hall, S.	} Killed in Action 24th Dec/15.
19482	"	Smith, J.H.	
17921	Cpl.	Pitson, E.J.	
19667	Pte	Crosley, H.W.	
19335	Pte.	Hodgkins, J.H.	Killed in Action 27/12/15
8724	L/C.	Ward, A.	- do - 28/12/15
16750	Pte	North, C.E.	} Wounded in Action 1st Dec't/15.
19613	"	Jones, P.J.	
21409	"	Reynolds, C	} Wounded in Action 2nd Dec't/15.
21314	"	Brailsford, W.	
8554	"	Jackson, G.	
15784	"	Collins, J.	
16782	"	Pearce, H.G.	} Wounded in Action 4th Dec't/15.
19796	"	Ward, G.H.	
15879	L/Sgt	Thackray, J.H.	Wounded in Action 11th Dec't/15
19629	Pte	Bolton, O.	} Wounded in Action 14th Dec't/15.
14499	"	Evans, W.	
13920	"	Miles, R.	Wounded in Action 15th Dec't/15

Roll of Casualties – Continued. (3)

Regtl No	Rank & Name		Remarks
13723	Pte	Bamford, J.	
15851	"	Coates, J.	
19652	Sgt	Heb, W.E.	
8893	"	Soskitt, G.E.	
15731	Pte	Beckley, J.	
17304	"	Sinkley, S.	
15086	"	Gatside, G.H.	Wounded in Action, 16th Sept 1915.
21660	"	Hartsme, H.	
19252	"	Hodgson, A.	
21663	"	Sharp, S.H.	
21219	"	Frost, G.A.	
3637	"	Ward, J.	
19284	L/Cpl	Lapping	
15681	Pte	Kane, J.V.	
19802	"	Holland, J.	
19859	"	Pessoll, J.	
21452	"	Hartley, P.B.	
14926	Sgt	Mellor, A.E.	
4616	Pte	Jones, J.	
1889	"	Naylor, J.	
19610	Cpl	Armstrong, W.	
4248	Pte	Cussell, W.	
15762	"	Chivers, H.	
18465	"	Fields, A.	
21056	"	Thorpe, S.	

Roll of Casualties — Continued. (4)

Regtl No.	Rank	Name	Remarks
17915	Pte	Kenny, J.W.	Wounded in Action 17th Dec't 1915.
3307	"	Cupitt, J.	
3311	"	Cupitt, B.	
21367	Cpl.	Ball, J.R.	Wounded in Action 21st Dec'r/1915
19830	Pte	Tutton, J.	
15638	"	Lees, J.G.	Wounded in Action 22nd Dec't 1915.
3159	"	Heatley, H.	
22737	"	Herbert, C.	
21284	"	Davies, R.O.	
19277	"	Farrell, M.	
15853	"	Saxon, H.	
14122	"	Taylor, E.	Wounded in Action 23rd December 1915.
15076	"	Soakell, H.	
19864	"	Smith, F.	
15177	"	Dyson, J.	
21545	"	Hopkinson, J.	
17909	"	Swaby, E.	
17469	"	Render, H.	
19647	L/Cpl.	Huddleston, W.	
21129	Pte	Breeze, J.	
14309	"	Roddis, B.	
7833	"	Goose, J.	
17821	"	Ballinger, H.	
17868	"	Tutton, A.	Wounded in Action 24th Dec'r/15.
21330	L/Cpl.	Beachill, A.	

Roll of Casualties — Continued. (5)

Regtl. No	Rank & Name		Remarks
4742	Pte	Jackson, A.	
19684	"	Jones, W.L.	
17249	"	Elliott, C.	Wounded in Action, 24th Dec'r/15.
20824	"	James, F.G.	
19759	"	Horne, A.	
3724	"	Simpson, F.S.	
16729	L/Cpl.	Coyne, J.	
19614	Pte.	Wright, J.	
9914	L/Cpl.	Barrett, E.W.	
19646	Pte	Wright, G.	
13824	"	Price, A.	Wounded in Action 27th Dec'r/15.
16802	"	Hammett, J.	
18520	"	Stenton, J.	
16816	"	Clifton, E.	Wounded in Action 29th Dec'r/15
13590	"	Lunn, W.H.	
4498	Sgt.	Connole, R.H.	
21213	Cpl	Hulley, J.	
4240	"	Coyne, P.	Wounded — Accidentally 19th Dec'r/15.
21223	"	Graham, W.	
15880	L/Cpl.	Cartwright, F.	
13640	Pte	Cassinelli, J.	
13701	"	Hopkins, I.H.	
4503	"	Russell, H.	Wounded Accidentally 26th Dec'r/15.

F Taylor Major
10th Bn York & Lancs. Regt.

10 The York Lancer.
Vol, 5

21/–

CONFIDENTIAL.

WAR DIARY

— of —

10th (S) Battn. YORK & LANCASTER REGT

From 2nd January 1916 to 4th Febry. 1916.

(Volume V)

WAR DIARY or INTELLIGENCE SUMMARY

Instructions regarding War Diaries and Intelligence Summaries are contained in F.S. Regs., Part II. and the Staff Manual respectively. Title Pages will be prepared in manuscript.

(Erase heading not required.)

Place	Date	Hour	Summary of Events and Information	
ARMENTIERES	2/1/16	9 p.m	Draft of 45 (forty-five) N.C.Os + men arrived.	App. I
ARMENTIERES	5/1/16	5 p.m	Battn. relieved 8 S.L.I. in trenches 70, 71, 72 + 73. — 8th Lincolns on our right, 10th Yorks on left.	App. II (Casualties)
ARMENTIERES	5/1/16	7 p.m	Draft of 17 (seventeen) NCOs + men arrived	App. I
ARMENTIERES	7/1/16	—	One Officer joined (2/Lt. Broadbent, C.S.M. having been granted Commission from 19th Scots/LS)	App. I
ARMENTIERES	9/1/16	7 p.m	Battn. relieved by 8 S.L.I in trenches as above.	
ARMENTIERES	12/1/16	5 p.m	Battn. went to trenches 67, 68 + 69, relieving Middlesex Regt. On our right 23rd Division, on left (trenches 70, 71, 72 + 73) 8th Lincoln Regt.	App. II (Casualties)
ARMENTIERES	16/1/16	7 p.m	Battn. relieved by 8 S.L.I. trenches 67, 68 + 69, as above.	App. II (Casualties)
ARMENTIERES	20/1/16	5 p.m	Battn. went into trenches 67, 68 + 69 to relieve 8 S.L.I. as above.	App. I
ARMENTIERES	24/1/16	7 p.m	Draft of 1 Offr. + 68 (other ranks arrived)	
ARMENTIERES	24/1/16	7 p.m	Battn. relieved by 8 S.L.I. trenches 67, 68 + 69, as above.	App. I
ARMENTIERES	26/1/16	—	Two Officers joined from 11th Yorks + Lancs. Regt.	App. I
ARMENTIERES	28/1/16	5 p.m	Battn. went into trenches 67, 68 + 69 to relieve 8 S.L.I. as above.	App. II (Casualties)
ARMENTIERES	31/1/16	—	One Officer joined (2/Lt. A.W. LAMOND granted Comm. from 1st Scots Guards, 17/1/16)	App. I
ARMENTIERES	4/1/16	7 p.m	Battn. relieved by 8th Lincs. Regt. from trenches 67, 68 + 69.	

(Appendix I)

10th (S) Bn York & Lancs. Regt.

Reinforcements.

Officers

5/1/16. 2/Lt. BROADBENT, H, granted Commn from C.S.M. as from 19th Dec't 1915.

22/1/16. 2/Lt. SYKES, C, joined Bn. from 11th Bn

26/1/16 Major TAYLOR, C.H. } joined Battn
26/1/16 2/Lt. SAMUELS, E. } from 11th Y & L

31/1/16 2/Lt LAMOND, A.W. granted Commn from Sgt. in Scots Guards (1st Bn) from 17/1/16.

Other ranks.

2/1/16   Forty five   from 11th Y & L.
5/1/16   Seventeen   — do —
22/1/16   Sixty eight   — do —

6th Febry/1916   2/Lt Bryan Lt & Adjt.
   10th Bn. York & Lancs Regt

(appendix II)

10th (S) Bn. York & Lancs. Regt.

CASUALTIES.

OFFICERS.

Rank & Name	Remarks
2/Lt PAYNE, F.E.	Wounded in Action – slightly – 24/1/16. To Field Ambulance for 3 or 4 days.

OTHER RANKS.

Regtl. No.	Rank & Name		Remarks
19695	Pte	Newton, E.	Killed in Action 3/1/16
19689	L/C	Perrett, A.	Killed in Action 5/1/16
17749	Pte	West, E.	Killed in Action 5/1/16
13057	"	Tannam, E.	
10882	"	Gibbs, G.	Killed in Action 14/1/16.
2539	"	Jackson, J.	KILLED in Action 27/1/16.

(2)

Regtl No.	Rank	Name	Remarks
9541	L/C	Nelson, R.	
19673	"	Egerton, C.	
11466	Pte	Timm, H.	
17543	"	Kitchen, C.	
17969	"	Wildgoose, A.	Wounded in Action, 5/1/16.
16944	"	Bellamy, J.	
3188	"	Ward, A.	
16925	"	Burley, J.	
11492	"	Henley, J.	
11633	"	Garnet, W.	
14719	"	Fisher, A.	
19624	L/C	Willman, W.	
18117	Pte	Abrahams, J.	Wounded in Action 8/1/16
15668	L/C	Chafer, A.	
19827	Pte	Sloan, S.	Wounded in Action, 14/1/1916
10257	L/C	Hinton, B.	
15773	Sgt	Swindall, S.	
21184	Pte	Millington, H.	Wounded in Action 15/1/16.
17946	Pte	Harvey, J.	Wounded in Action, 21/1/16.
19825	"	Robinson, R.	
19602	Pte	Williams, J.	Wounded in Action 24/1/16

- 3 -

Regtl No.	Rank	Name	Remarks
13845	Sgt	Callaghan B.J.	Wounded in Action 27/1/16
15923	Pte	Hancock, N.	Wounded in Action 29/1/16
21229	Pte	Sassant, J.	Wounded in Action 31/1/16
20714	Pte	Buchanan, H.	Wounded in Action 2/2/16
14157	L/C	Duggan, M.	}
14742	"	Baugh, J.	}
16875	Pte	Lunn, S.	}
18117	"	Abrahams, J.	}
21079	"	Rheam, A.	}
19416	"	Bacon, S.S.	} Wounded in Action 3/2/16.
16477	"	Hinchcliffe, J.	}
4636	"	Spellman, J.	}
16770	"	Atkinson, G.	}
13627	"	Eales, H.	}
17446	"	Dillon, M.	}
16918	"	Stones,	}
16945	"	Lee.	}
21440	"	Bates,	}
16518	"	Marsh,	}
11075	"	Kaye,	}

6th Feby/16.

H. Dyson Lt. + Adjt
10th Bn. York & Lancs. Regt

CONFIDENTIAL.

WAR DIARY

— of —

10th (S) Battn. YORK & LANC^{r} REG^{T}

From 4th Febry. 1916 to 29th Febry. 1916.

(VOLUME VI)

Army Form C. 2118

WAR DIARY
or
INTELLIGENCE SUMMARY

(Erase heading not required.)

Instructions regarding War Diaries and Intelligence Summaries are contained in F.S. Regs., Part II. and the Staff Manual respectively. Title Pages will be prepared in manuscript.

Place	Date	Hour	Summary of Events and Information	Remarks and references to Appendices
ARMENTIERES	4/2/16	7 p.m.	Battalion went into Reserve of Brigade.	
ARMENTIERES	7/2/16	5 p.m.	Battalion moved from "Reserve" Billets to ordinary Rest Billets.	
ARMENTIERES	7/2/16	7 p.m.	Draft of 35 (Thirty-five) N.C.Os. & Men arrived. One Officer joined.	App. I App. I
ARMENTIERES	10/2/16	—		
ARMENTIERES	13/2/16	6 a.m.	Battn. went into trenches 83 to 89 inclusive, to relieve 9th K.O.Y.L.I. on our right, 8th Somerset L.I. on our left 9th Division.	App. I App. I
ARMENTIERES	14/2/16	9 p.m.	Draft of 33 (Thirty-three) N.C.Os. & Men arrived.	App. I
ARMENTIERES	17/2/16	7 p.m.	Draft of 18 (eighteen) N.C.Os. & Men arrived.	App. I
ARMENTIERES	19/2/16	6 a.m.	Battn. relieved by 4th Bn. Middlesex Regt. from front line of trenches 83 to 89 inclusive, 10 York & Lanc. Regt. moving into Subsidiary line of above trenches.	App. II
ARMENTIERES	22/2/16	6 a.m.	Battn. relieved by 8th Bn. Somerset L.I. from Subsidiary line of trenches 83 to 89 inclusive, 10 York & Lanc. Regt. moving into Support of above trenches.	App. II
ARMENTIERES	24/2/16	—	One Officer joined.	App. I
ARMENTIERES	25/2/16	6 a.m.	Battn. relieved from Supports of trenches 83 to 89 inclusive by 1st Lincoln Regt. (62nd Brigade) 10th York & Lanc. Regt. moving back to rest billets Armentieres.	App. II App. I
ARMENTIERES	26/2/16	9 p.m.	Draft of 30 (Thirty) N.C.Os. & Men arrived.	App. I

10th (S) Bn. York & Lanc. Regt.
1/3/16

App. I

10th (S) Bn. York & Lancs. Regt.

Reinforcements during February 1916.

Officers.

10/2/1916.	Captain WILLIS, A.J.,	Arrived from 11th York & Lancs. Regt.
24/2/1916	2/Lieut. NICHOLSON, C.A.J.	— ditto —

Other Ranks.

7th Feb/16.	Thirty-five	Arrived from Base, Etaples
14th Feb/16.	Thirty-three	— ditto —
17th Feb/16.	Eighteen.	— ditto —
26th Feb/16.	Thirty.	— ditto —

pr Comdg. 10th (S) Bn. York & Lancs. Regt.

1st March. 1916.

App. II

10th (S) Bn. York & Lanc+ Regt.

CASUALTIES during February, 1916.

OFFICERS
_____

— NIL —
_____

OTHER RANKS

Date.	In Trenches.	Working parties. Resting, etc	Remarks.
12/2/16.		17251 Pte. Dodd, G.W. 14435 L/c. Hallsworth, W. 22714 Pte. Nettleship, J.H.	Wounded.
12/2/16.		22894 Pte. Harrison, W.A.	Killed.
17/2/16.	2870 Pte. Woodmansey, F.S. 19795 " Tighe, L.W. 19994 " Allott, S.		Wounded
18/2/16.	21075 Pte. West, H. 15889 " Baker, C.H. 15922 L/c. Anderson, J. 21428 Pte. Webster, J. 22732 " Norman, J.		Wounded
21/2/16.	19726 L/c. Attack, J.		Wounded
22/2/16	16494 Pte. Holmes, J.		Wounded.
24/2/16.	3561 L/c. Wigglesworth, A.		Wounded
29/2/16.		17431 Pte. Jubb, J. 15681 " Kane, J.V.	Killed
29/2/16.		16849 Pte. Gladhall, J.G. 20643 " Lloyd, J. 16026 " Mellor, J.	Wounded.

1st March 1916.

for Comdg. 10th (S) Bn. York & Lanc+ Regt.

CONFIDENTIAL

WAR DIARY OF THE

10th (Ser) Battn York & Lancaster Regt.

1st of March 1916

to

1st of April 1916

— (Volume VII) —

WAR DIARY or INTELLIGENCE SUMMARY

Army Form C. 2118

Place	Date	Hour	Summary of Events and Information	Remarks and references to Appendices
ARMENTIERES	1/3/16		(Base at Rest) Battn. reoccupying rest billets. H.Q. at 60 Rue de la Gare. Camel.	
"	2/3/16		(Base relieve) Battn. moved into Blue Billets, relieving 10th O.Y.L.I. H.Q. at 20 13th Faid Rube.	
"	4/3/16		Hostile shelling in town. 9 O.Rs wounded including R.S.M. French S.	
"	5/3/16		Battn. relieved 8 S.R. in subsidiary line (night relief) occupying from left of LILLE Road to TISSAGE.	app. II
"	8/3/16		Battn. relieved E. LINCS. in front line and supports occupying from T64 to TYLINTERINE.	
"	10/3/16		Draft of 51 NCOs and other ranks arrived from Base.	
"	12/3/16		2nd Lieut. SMITH. R.A. joined from 11th (Res) Battn.	app. I
"	13/3/16		Major FRANK TAYLOR killed in action.	app. I
"	14/3/16		Battn. relieved in T64, T68 by 4 MIDDX. and in T40 and T41 by 2 LINCS, moving into Blue Billets. H.Q. at 20 13th Faid Rube. 2 O.Rs killed in action.	app. II
"	17/3/16		2nd Lieut. QUANCE L.A. joined from 11th (Res) Battn.	app. II
LA CRECHE	20/3/16		Battn. moved by route march to LA CRECHE occupying rest billets.	app. II
STRAZEELE	21/3/16		Battn. moved by route march to STRAZEELE occupying rest billets.	app. I
"	24/3/16		Draft of 23 NCOs and others arrived from Base.	
"	25/3/16		Lieut. GROVES. S.J.S. joined from 11th (Res) Battn.	
ALLONVILLE	1/4/16		Battn. moved by route march to and entrained at GODWAESVELDE detraining at LONGEAU and proceeded by route march to ALLONVILLE occupying rest billets. (Transfer to XIII Corps. Fourth Army).	app. I

Bradford Hadyn
10th (Service) Bn. York & Lancaster Reg.

App. I

10th (Ser) Battn. York & Lancaster Regt.

REINFORCEMENTS joining Battn during MARCH 1916.

OFFICERS.

Rank	Name	Date of joining	Remarks
2/Lieut	SMITH R.A.	12/3/1916	From 11th (Res) Bn
"	QUANCE A.L.	14/3/1916	"
Lieut	GROVES S.J.S.	25/3/1916	"

OTHER RANKS.

Date	Number	Remarks
10/3/1916	51	From 21 I.B.D.
24/3/1916	23	"

A Broadbent Lt.Col.
10th (Service) Bn. York & Lancaster Regt.

App II

10th (Ser) Battn York & Lancaster Regt

CASUALTIES incurred during MARCH 1916

OFFICERS

Major FRANK TAYLOR – Killed in action – 13/3/1916

OTHER RANKS.

Date	In trenches	Working parties. resting. etc	Remarks.
1/3/1916		14560 Pte Curry E. 3114 " Woodward J.	} Wounded.
4/3/1916		4297 RSM French S. 10634 L/Cpl McManus J. 2854 Pte Richardson E.C. 17748 " Halligan J. 19606 " Eage R. 13693 L/Cpl Chapman E. 19491 Pte Matthias A. 22811 " Pickersgill W.	} Wounded
6/3/1916	16733 Pte Duckworth F. (self inflicted) 17896 Pte Birch J.		} Wounded
8/3/1916	19660 " Brannon J.		Wounded
9/3/1916	21295 " Heenan W. 16755 " Russell J.		} Wounded
11/3/1916	3093 " Wigham E.		Wounded
12/3/1916	17927 " Heath H. 14951 " Hutton H.		} Wounded
12/3/1916	1651 " Jenkinson W.		Wounded
14/3/1916	16005 " Bryan J. 21484 " Haywood E.W. 10694 " Studd J.		} Wounded
	15411 " Blackburn E. 13886 " Wilson W.		} Killed
15/3/1916		18858 Pte Knight C.H.	Wounded.

H Bradshaw Lt Adj
10th (Service) Bn. York & Lancaster Regt

CONFIDENTIAL

10th (Ser.) Batt. York & Lancaster Regt.

— WAR DIARY —

from 1st April 1916

to 30th April 1916

Volume VIII

WAR DIARY
or
INTELLIGENCE SUMMARY

(Erase heading not required.)

Army Form C. 2118

Place	Date	Hour	Summary of Events and Information	Remarks and references to Appendices
ALLONVILLE	2/7/16		Battn in rest billets	
BUIRE sur Ancre	3/7/16		Battn proceeded by route march to BUIRE occupying rest billets	
MEAULTE	4/7/16		Battn went into Trenches in front of MEAULTE relieving 11th Border Regt.	
"	5/7/16		Battn relieved in Trenches by 1st East Yorks, and occupy close shelter billets MEAULTE	
BUIRE sur Ancre	9/7/16		Battn proceeded by route march to BUIRE occupying rest billets.	
"	14/7/16		Draft of Eighteen NCOs & Men arrived from Base	Appx I
MEAULTE	15/7/16		Battn proceeded by route march to MEAULTE occupying close billets. Hostile shelling in village. 1 OR killed and 2 severely wounded, since dying of wounds.	} Appx II
LA NEUVILLE	22/7/16		Relieved in close billets by 1st Lincs. Battn proceeded by route march to LA NEUVILLE occupying rest billets.	
"	24/7/16		2 Officers arrived from Base	Appx I
"	28/7/16		Draft of 33 ORs arrived from Base	Appx I

A Broadhead
Major.
10th (Service) Bn. York & Lancaster

Appendix I

10th (Service) Bn. York & Lancaster Regt.

Reinforcements joining Battn. during April 1916.

OFFICERS

Rank and Name	Date of Joining	Remarks
Capt. di Marco. P. H.	24/4/16	From 11th Res. Battn.
2 Lieut. Morton Smith, F.	24/4/16	—

OTHER RANKS.

Date	Number	Remarks
14/4/1916	18 N.C.Os. and Men.	From 21 I.B.D.
28/4/1916	33 N.C.Os. and Men.	From 21 I.B.D.

H Broadbent Lt & Adjt.
10th (Service) Bn. York & Lancaster Regt.

Appendix II

10th (Service) Bn. York & Lancaster Regt.

CASUALTIES incurred during APRIL 1916.

OFFICERS.

— NIL —

OTHER RANKS.

Date	In Trenches	Working Parties, Resting, etc.	Remarks
6/4/16	23196 Pte. Smallman, F.		Wounded.
14/4/16		3530 Pte. Wrigley, H.	Wounded.
15/4/16	21612 Pte. Crawford, H.		Died of Wounds
	14849 — Bennett, A.		— do —
	16841 L.Cpl. Rushforth, J.		Killed.
14/4/16	15475 Cpl. Calvert, H.		Wounded accidentally (to duty)
	14958 — Rhodes, J.H.C.		Wounded accidental
	15423 Pte. Young, A.		— do —
	15311 — Barker, H.		— do —
	19425 — Acklam, J.		Wounded
	14566 — Sewter, R.		— do —
19/4/16	5499 Pte. Rodgers, F.W.		— do —

H. Broadbent
Lt. Adjt.
10th (Service) Bn. York & Lancaster Regt.

Confidential.

10th (Ser) Battn York & Lanc Regt.

— War Diary —

from 1st May 1916

to 30th May 1916.

Volume IX

Officer i/c

New Army Inf'y Section No.2.

Herewith War Diary of this Battalion for the month of May 1916, forwarded to you in accordance with Field Service Regulations Part 11. Section 140.

A Broadbent Lieut Adjt

Comdg. 10th Battn. York & Lanc. Regt.

3/6/16.

Army Form C. 2118

WAR DIARY
or
INTELLIGENCE SUMMARY
(Erase heading not required.)

Instructions regarding War Diaries and Intelligence Summaries are contained in F.S. Regs., Part II. and the Staff Manual respectively. Title Pages will be prepared in manuscript.

Place	Date	Hour	Summary of Events and Information	Remarks and references to Appendices
LA NEUVILLE	1/5/16		Battn occupying red. billets (New Rest. Area).	
BRAY sur SOMME	2/5/16		Battn proceeded by route march to BRAY sur SOMME relieving 9 K.O.Y.L.I. in Close billets (Working Party Area)	
MEAULTE	12/5/16		Battn proceeded by route march to MEAULTE relieving 9 K.O.Y.L.I. in Bde Reserve occupying close billets.	
	14/5/16		Capt. R.W. O'Guelin's joined Battn. Battn relieved 8 Som. L.I. in Trenches from z5-x26/1 x 26/5 having on right in Tambou 8 R. LINES.	— Appx I.
	16/5/16		2 O.Rs killed	= Appx II
	18/5/16		1 O.R. killed	= Appx II
	20/5/16		1 O.R. killed	— Appx II
	21/5/16		Draft of 20 ORs arrived from 96 & 21. I.B.D.	
BUIRE	22/5/16		Relieved in Trenches by 12.N.F. and proceeded by route march to BUIRE occupying Reserve billets.	
LA NEUVILLE	23/5/16		Battn proceeded by route march to LA NEUVILLE occupying red. billets. (New Rest Area) 2nd Lieut D.H. DRAKE joined from 11th (2nd Res) Battn.	— Appx I

HBroadbent Lieut Adj: F.S.
O/C 10th Bn York Lancaster Regt.

Appendix II.

10th (Ser) Bn. YORK & LANCASTER Regiment.

CASUALTIES incurred during MAY 1916.

OFFICERS. Nil.

OTHER RANKS.

Date.	In Trenches.	Working Parties, Resting, etc.	Remarks.
1/5/16.		21618 L/C. Shaw, J.W. (Bde. Mining Section).	Wounded.
4/5/16.		2927 Pte. Coates, G.H. (Bde. Mining Section)	Wounded.
13/5/16.		19699 Pte. Petty, F.	Wounded.
16/5/16.	16729 Cpl. Coyne, J.) 21641 Pte. Phillips, E.) 21224 : Partington, J.S.)		Wounded.
	20651 L/C. Richings, E.M.		Killed.
	15688 Pte. Eason, W.		Killed.
17/5/16.	11472 Pte. Hendley, T.		Wounded (to duty)
	18371 Pte. Percival, H.) 23271 : Hayes, J.)		Wounded.
18/5/16.	10524 Pte. Sutcliffe, W.) 17857 : Christmas, T.)		Wounded.
	19245 Pte. Sefton, H.		Killed.
19/5/16.	19742 Pte. Dunning, F.) 14616 : Boid, T.)		Wounded (to duty)
	15302 Pte. Chilton, A.		Wounded.
20/5/16.	15927 Pte. Hopkinson, G.) 23248 : Hackett, T.)		Wounded.
	19612 L/C. Ince, W.		Killed.
21/5/16.	17511 Pte. Turtle, J.C.) 13727 : Fawcett, A.)		Wounded.
22/5/16.	16526 L/Sgt. Duncan, T.A.) 22790 L/C. Rowley, R.J.)		Wounded.

F.Broadwater /Lieut/

for OC 10th Bn York & Lancs Regt.

Appendix I.

10th (Ser) Bn. YORK & LANCASTER Regiment.

REINFORCEMENTS arriving during the month of MAY 1916.

OFFICERS.   2.

    Captain R.W. MULLINS arrived from 11th (Res) Battn. 12/5/16.
    2/Lieut. D.H. DRAKE arrived from 11th (Res) Battn. 23/5/16.

OTHER RANKS.   20.

    Twenty N.C.Os and Men arrived from No. 21 I.B. Depot 21/5/16.

------xxxxx------

H Broadbent Lieut Adjt
for OC 10th Bn York & Lanc Regt.

CONFIDENTIAL.

THE

WAR DIARY

OF

10th Bn. York and Lancaster Regt.

from 1st June 1916

To 30th June 1916

Volumme X

Army Form C. 2118

WAR DIARY
or
INTELLIGENCE SUMMARY
(Erase heading not required.)

Instructions regarding War Diaries and Intelligence Summaries are contained in F.S. Regs., Part II. and the Staff Manual respectively. Title Pages will be prepared in manuscript.

Place	Date	Hour	Summary of Events and Information	Remarks and references to Appendices
LA NEUVILLE BUIRE	1/6/16		Bn. in rest billets	
	2/6/16		Bn. proceeded by Route March to BUIRE, occupying rest billets and relieving 12 N.F.	
	4/6/16		Grenade accident. 3 O.R.s wounded.	
	6/6/16		2/Lt. C.H. Graven and 44 O.R.s joined Bn. from Base.	
	7/6/16		Lt. D.D. Hawley joined Bn. from Base.	
MEAULTE	11/8/16		Bn. proceeded by route march to take up intermediate line in front of MEAULTE relieving 9ROYL. H.Q. at MEAULTE. 5 Sgts. 4 MIDDX line.	
			2/Lt. Pirie.	
	13/6/16		Major J.H. Ragaway joined from N. Stafford Rgt.	
			Capt. C.D.S.G. McGilton joined from Base.	
TRENCHES	15/6/16		Bn. relieved 8 S.L.I. in Divisional line.	
			in intermediate line. Dur/Lieut Gallon 5 S.L.I. taking up position mentioned.	
			Lt. Col. C.H. Taylor left Bn. this being invalided to England on G.H.Q. instructions. The command of the Bn. being taken by Lt. Col Ragaway T.H. from E. York Regt.	
	17/6/16		1 O.R. killed. Capt. T.B.O. Tunnill joined from E. York Regt.	
	19/6/16		Capt P.H. du Marco wounded.	
LA NEUVILLE	20/6/16		Bn. relieved in front line by 1st June Regt. and proceeded by motorbuses to LANEUVILLE rest billets. 2 offrs. 2 O.R.s a Military and 2/Lt. J. Douglas joined from Base.	
VILLE	27/6/16		Bn. proceeded to VILLE and occupied reserve billets. Draft of 60 O.R.s joined from Base.	

2076.

J. Broadbent Lt. Adjt.

10th (S) Bn. York & Lanc. Regt.

APPENDIX.

10th (Ser) Bn. York & Lancaster Regiment.

CASUALTIES incurred during the month of JUNE 1916.

Date.	In Trenches.	Working Parties, Resting, etc.	Remarks.
4/6/1916		14719 Pte. Fisher, A.	Wounded accidentally. Since died of wounds.
		11004 Pte. Preston, J.	Wounded accidentally.
		15402 Pte. Gelder, J.	Wounded accidentally (To duty).
9/6/1916	19719 L/C. Williams, H.		Wounded. With Bde. Mining Sec.
13/6/1916	15058 Sgt. Hodgkinson, W.		Wounded.
	19696 L/S. Oates, N.		Wounded.
16/6/1916	21501 Pte. Sims, G.		Killed.
17/6/1916.	21483 Pte. Proberts, W.		Killed.
18/6/1916.	24003 Pte. Jackson, G.		Wounded (To duty).
19/6/1916.	Capt. P.H. di MARCO.		Wounded.

SICK WASTAGE.

Officers   Nil.   Other Ranks.   To   Field Amb.   29
                                        From Field Amb.   15

                                        Total Wastage   14.

REINFORCEMENTS arriving during the month of JUNE 1916.

Officers.		Other Ranks.
2/Lt. C.H. GODWIN joined	6/6/1916.	44 Other Ranks joined 6/6/1916.
2/Lt. D.D. HAWLEY joined	7/6/1916.	60 Other Ranks joined 27/6/1916.
Lt-Col. J.H. RIDGWAY joined from North Staffordshire Regiment	15/6/1916.	
Capt. J.B.O. TRIMBLE joined from East Yorkshire Regiment	17/6/1916.	
Capt. C.L.St.G. McClellan joined	15/6/1916.	
2/Lt. A. HOCKLY joined	20/6/1916.	
2/Lt. J. DOUGLAS joined	20/6/1916.	

Copy No. App. I
SECRET.

OPERATION ORDERS

By Lieut-Col. J.H. Ridgway,
Comdg. 10th (S) Bn. York & Lancaster Regiment.
23rd June 1916.

Map Reference   1:10,000.

NOTE.-   Zero is the hour of assault.
Z Day is the day of assault.
Days previous to the assault are allotted a letter of the alphabet, i.e. U Day is the 5th day before the assault.

----

1. (a) The 21st Division with 50th Bde. attached is ordered to seize and consolidate

   <u>First Objective</u>   FRICOURT FARM - TRENCH JUNCTION X 28 c 8.7 - CRUCIFIX TRENCH - BIRCH TREE WOOD.

   <u>Second Objective</u>   X 29 b 5.0 (joining with 7th Div.) - X 28 c 6565 - QUADRANGLE Trench to Trench Junction X 22 b 6565.

   (b) The 7th Division on right is ordered to capture MAMETZ and to occupy the line S 23 b 5032 - X 29 b 5.6.

   (c) The 34th Division on left to seize and consolidate

   <u>First Objective</u>   BIRCH TREE WOOD (exclusive) - BAILLIFF WOOD.

   <u>Second Objective</u>   X 22 b 6565 and line to the North and West of CONTALMAISON.

   <u>Third Objective</u>   CONTALMAISON and line running N.W. from ACID DROP COPSE.

   (NOTE - The clearing of FRICOURT and FRICOURT WOOD is being undertaken as a separate operation after the main attack has progressed).

2. The 63rd Brigade will therefore seize and consolidate the following objectives

   (a) <u>First Objective.</u>

   <u>4th Middlesex Regt.</u> - FRICOURT FARM - X 28 c 8.7 - bend of Trench at X 28 a 5005 inclusive with
   Advanced Posts in RAILWAY ALLEY and COPSE, up to Railway Line about X 28 b 1.3 inclusive.

   <u>8th Somerset L.I.</u> - from bend of trench at X 28 a 5005 exclusive - CRUCIFIX TRENCH to X 27 b 7841 with
   Advanced Posts from X 28 b 1.3 exclusive to S. end of SHELTER WOOD exclusive.

   (b) <u>Second Objective.</u>

   <u>10th York & Lanc. Regt.</u> - X 29 b 5.6 (joining 7th Division) to X 23 d 1500 (if the ground at X 29 b 5.6 is not occupied by 7th Division when this line is reached it will be held by 10th York & Lanc. Regt. with bombers pushed down CLIFF Trench) with
   Advanced Posts on the line X 30 a 0.6 - X 23 d 6.0.

8th Lincoln Regt. - X 23 d 1500 - QUANDRANGLE to X 23 c 6565 (where QUADRANGLE TRENCH crosses MAMETX - CONTALMAISON ROAD) inclusive, with Advance d Posts on the line X 23 d 6.0 - Railway to X 23 d 2590 (this should include a block in QUADRANGLE TRENCH).

3. The dividing line between Battalions to the first objective will be a line drawn from the point of junction in the assembly trench to the Eastern end of LOZENGE WOOD and from there to point X 28 a 5005. The dividing line between Battalions to the 2nd objective will be X 28 a 5005, RAILWAY COPSE (inclusive to 10th York & Lanc. Regt), Railway to the point where it enters BOTTOM WOOD - X 23 d 1500.

4. The 50th Brigade is attacking simultaneously on the right of 4th Middlesex Regt. (10th West Yorks Regt. will be on right of 4th Middlesex Regt.) with the object of

(a) Clearing the front system of German Trenches and that part of FRICOURT between the boundaries, on South F 4 a 5.3 - F 3 b 5.3 on North C 27 c 3025 - X 27 d 9540, on EAST LONELY COPSE inclusive SUNKEN ROAD - WELL LANE and trench running S.W. from Point 5241.

(b) Occupying a position in the neighbourhood of RED COTTAGE to protect the right flank of 63rd Brigade in the SUNKEN ROAD.

5. The attack will be preceded by a 5 days bombardment, in the course of which the wire is to be cut and trenches destroyed up to and including the line of the Second Objective.

6. Further orders will be issued as to moving up to the trenches prior to the assault.

7. Communication Trenches will be used as follows:-

    UP   -   LINDUM STREET - HUNTLEY STREET.

    DOWN -   KING'S AVENUE.
                QUEEN'S AVENUE diverted (for casualties).
                STONEHAVEN STREET.

8. Brigade Hd Qrs. will be at junction of 101 STREET and SHUTTLE LANE.

10th York & Lanc. Regt.

Hd Qrs. at Junction of 100 and SURREY STREETS.
A. and C. Coys. in SURREY STREET from KING'S CROSS to QUEEN'S Avenue, C. Coy taking from 100 STREET to QUEEN'S Avenue inclusive, and A. Coy. from a point 40 yards on the right of LINDUM STREET to KING'S CROSS.
B. and D. Coys. will be in MARESCHAL STREET, B. Coy. from KING'S CROSS to LINDUM STREET, and D. Coy. from LINDUM STREET TO QUEEN'S AVENUE.
Headquarters, consisting of Battn. Bombers, Snipers, H.Q. Signallers, Orderlies, R.G. Squad, will be in open space between A. and C. Coys. Blocking party will be in SURREY STREET on extreme right of A. Coy. Order from the right: Bombers, Snipers, Signallers, and Orderlies.

9. The formation in the attack will be as follows:-

```
_____                              _____
_____                              _____
_____    C. Coy.                   _____   A. Coy.
_____                              _____


_____ )                           ( _____
_____ )  B. Coy.                  ( _____
_____ )                           ( _____


_____ )                           ( _____
_____ )  D. Coy.                  ( _____
_____ )                           ( _____
```

Hd. Qrs: Battn. Bombers, Signallers, Snipers, R.G. Squad.
Lewis Guns will be attached to their Companies.

10. During the Advance, O.C. D. Coy., 10th York & Lancs. will detach one platoon under Lt.   to seize and consolidate the N.E. end of FRICOURT WOOD. This Platoon will make for their objective after passing through the 4th Middlesex Regt; this party to be fully provided with picks and shovels from those allotted to D. Coy. If the barrage of fire is still on the N.E. Corner of Wood as Battalion advances, this platoon will wait and advance immediately it is lifted.

11. The party of 60 men already detailed, under Lt. Drake, will be held in readiness to block all trenches on the line X 27 c 3025 - X 27 d 0542. Tools and explosives, as already detailed, will be provided. This party will follow immediately after the last wave of the 4th Middlesex Regt.

12. In the event of the 7th Division not having reached the high ground X 29 b 5.6, A. Coy. will detail a platoon to hold that ground, with bombers pushed down CLIFF Trench.

13. Two Stokes Guns will be attached to Battn. Hd Qrs after the Battn. has passed through the 4th Middlesex Regt.

14. All lines of this Battalion will start the attack direct from their Assembly Trenches.

15. The Battalion will move into the Assembly Trenches on the night Y/Z. All wire in front of MARESCHAL STREET will be removed on the night Y/Z.

16. Infantry will not carry packs. The haversack, water bottle and a waterproof sheet will be carried on the back.
    In addition:-
    220 rounds, 2 sandbags and 2 grenades per man will be carried.
    Gas helmets will be rolled up on the head.

17. Compass bearings will be taken on the flanks of objectives, and will be made known to all Officers.

18. A tracing of Artillery barrages will be passed round Companies, who will mark them on their maps, with times at which they will lift.
    All ranks must thoroughly understand the times of the different barrages, and realize that each barrage must be followed up as close

- 4 -

19. Particular attendtion is drawn to para 17 Div. O.O. regarding Re-bombardment, copies of which will be issued to Companies.

20. Regimental Aif Post will be established at the Junction of QUEEN'S Avenue and SURREY Street.
Advanced Dressing Station at QUEEN'S REDOUBT.

21. B. Coy. will garrison with one platoon and one Lewis Gun Supporting Point No. 16 at X 22 b 9045 (N.E. Corner of BOTTOM WOOD). This point will be taken over when completed by the R.E. and Pioneers. This point must be held at all costs.

22. Battn. Hd Qrs after commencement of operations will move to X 27 d 2.3, thence to X 28 b 1½.1½, thence to X 29 b 0.5½.

23. A dump of S.A.A. and Grenades etc. will be formed at the S.W. Corner of RAILWAY COPSE.
D. Coy. will detail 24 men to carry 192 drums Lewis Gun Ammunition (for which bags will be provided) to the Dump. They will also detail a party of 30 men to carry forward 15 boxes S.A.A., which they will draw from Battn. Sgt-Major in the Assembly Trench at Corner of LINDUM STREET and MARESCHAL Street.
D. Coy. will also detail 20 men to carry forward 1,000 Mills grenades in buckets. These will be drawn from R.S.M. at same place, and carried forward to Dump.
The Snipers will draw 5 boxes S.A.A. from R.S.M. at same place on their way up to Assembly Trenches, and carry these forward on advance to same dump. All these parties will be under Officers or suitable N.C.Os.
D. Coy. will detail one suitable N.C.O. to remain in charge of Dump.
Coys. will draw on the dump when necessary.
The carrying party after dumping these stores will rejoin their Companies.
It is most important that all ranks should understand the necessity for economy in the use of grenades.

24. A Brigade Reserve of S.A.A., Grenades, will be formed in the SUNKEN ROAD at place to be labelled.

25. Orders will be issued later with regard to

        100 rounds extra S.A.A. perman.
          2 Grenades,
          2 sandbags,
        500 Flares,   per Brigade.
        150 picks,   per Battalion.
        150 shovels,

which will be distributed at VILLE.

26. All prisoners will be escorted back to A.P.M. in BECOURT Valley (F 2 c S.W.). Escorts which will be arranged by O.C. Coys. will be in the proportion of 5% of prisoners. All documents etc. will be taken from them at once, and handed over to A.P.M. Braces and belts will be taken from them. A receipt will be obtained from A.P.M. on handing them over.

27. F.O.Os will put up a black square about 1 foot to mark their positions.

28. On reaching the 2nd Objective, Patrols with a Lewis Gun will be immediately sent forward by the two leading Companies, to cover the remainder of Battalion, who will be consolidating the objective, and to give warning of impending Counter-attacks. The right Company is responsible for gaining touch with 7th Division.
B. Coy., less a Platoon, under Capt. Trimble, will form Outpost Line immediately his Company is reorganized after reaching objective, and will gain touch with 7th Division. This Company will relieve the patrols who will rejoin their Companies.

29. Gas and smoke will be used, if wind is favourable. Gas will be used on one of the nights previous to attack. On Z day (if wind is favourable) whiffs of gas will be turned on 15 minutes before Zero, on portion of line between our right and TAMBOUR.

30. Flags will be issued to Coys. on scale of one per Platoon to mark their positions during advance. These will be red and yellow on first day, red and blue on second, and red and yellow on third day. Flags for second and third days will be sent up on the previous nights.

31. Three Aeroplanes will be detailed for Contact Work. Type: Morane Parasol. Special Markings: A broad band under left hand plane. One Contact Aeroplane will be in the air at a time.

32. On Z day Flares will be lit by leading Coys. to communicate their positions as follows:-

    (a) On reaching second objective.

    (b) All along the line of the most forward Infantry at the following hours:- 9.0.a.m., 1.0 p.m., 5.0 p.m., 9.0 p.m. These flares will be fired in the following way:- 3 Flares will be used and fired in a row at 3 or 4 paces interval; fire one flare, ½ minute interval, fire second flare; ½ minute interval, fire third flare. These must be carried by Officers and N.C.Os and will be well distributed in case of casualties.

33. All Officers and N.C.O's will take Command of all men in their immediate neighbourhood, irrespective of Unit.

34. A surplus Kit and Store Dump has been formed at No. 20 Rue PONT NOYELLES, in LA NEUVILLE. This Dump is marked with white notice board with black letters. All Regimental Stores which are surplus to the authorised weight load of wagons will be dumped at this dump by 5.0 p.m. V. day.

In this category are included all Officers' Kits surplus to authorised weight, viz. 35 lb., and such other kits as Sewing Machines, and gramaphones, extra cooking utensils etc.

At the same dump, but in separate barns will be left all packs. These will be dumped by noon on X Day.

All bulk stores and everything which can be evacuated to Salvage, and which is not included in para 2 above will be dumped at Salvage dump by 5.0 p.m. on V. Day.

A guard over pack dump will be provided by 4th Middlesex Regt.

35. All ranks going into assembly trenches will carry rations issued that day, and iron rations. All water bottles to be filled, and men are warned that there is no certainty when next supply of water will be available, and that every care should be taken to husband their supply.

36. All ration parties on night Z/A will draw food etc. from Cookers at point corner of LOZENGE WOOD and SUNKEN ROAD. Instructions for other days will be issued later.

37.

37. No papers, documents, etc. will be taken into trenches, except 1:20,000 map. All provisional Battalion Orders issued are to be destroyed on receipt of these.

(Sd) H. Broadbent, Lieut. & Adjt.
for O.C. 10th (S) Bn. York & Lancaster Regiment.

Distribution.	Copy No.
63rd Inf. Bde.	1
Battn. H.Q.	2
do.	3
A. Coy.	4
B. Coy.	5
C. Coy.	6
D. Coy.	7
Transport Officer	8
Quartermaster	9
Signalling Officer	10
Bombing Officer	11
War Diary	12

SECRET.

AMENDMENT NO 1 to OPERATION ORDERS, dated 23/6/1916.

Reference Operation Orders dated 23rd June 1916. Paras 1 (b), and 2 (b) are cancelled. The following is substituted.

A new German Trench has been dug as follows:-

QUADRANGLE Trench X 23 c 4565 - Northern edge of BOTTOM WOOD X 28 b 9127, to Railway Alley X 28 d 8050.

In consequence,

the main second objective of the 21st Division as given in the above order is cancelled and the following substituted:

Second Objective, 63rd Inf. Bde.

X 29 b 5.6 (to connect with 7th Division) - thence along Northern edge of BOTTOM WOOD by Works 16/13 to new trench X 29 a 1.8 - along new trench to QUANDRANGLE Trench X 23 c 4.5 (exclusive).

Second Objective, 64th Inf. Bde.

Junction of new trench and QUANDRANGLE TRENCH X 23 c 4.5 (incl.) - along QUANDRANGLE Trench to original Northern limit. Responsible for blocking QUANDRANGLE Trench to the East.

The following advanced line will be occupied at once, and consolidated as soon as main objective has been consolidated, viz.

X 29 b 5.6 - Work 17 QUANDRANGLE WOOD to Work 18.
X 23 d 0548 (inclusive).

23/6/1916.

(Sd) H. Broadbent, Lieut. & Adjt.
for Lieut-Col. Comdg. 10th York & Lancaster Regt.

Appendix No. 1.

SECRET.

Instructions as to Re-Bombardment.

(a) If any point of the enemy's lines holds up our Infantry advance to such an extent that it is necessary to bombard again that portion of the enemy's defence, application for re-bombardment will be made to Divisional Headquarters.

(b) The Divisional Commander will fix the zero hour at which the re-bombardment will commence.
The normal re-bombardment will last 30 minutes, of which the last five minutes will be intensive. The bombardment will lift at D.30, at which hour the Infantry will assault.
It is to be thoroughly understood by all ranks that the only orders regarding re-bombardment that will be issued will be a message naming the hour fixed for zero (i.e. the hour at which the bombardment will commence).

(c) In the event of it being found impossible by the Artillery to begin the re-bombardment at the hour fixed as zero, either the re-bombardment will begin as early as possible after zero hour and cease at 30 minutes after zero, the last five minutes being intensive; or a fresh zero hour will be fixed.

Copy of 21 Div. O.O. para 17.

ADDITION to OPERATION ORDERS No. 1, dated 23/6/1916.

1. The possibility of a collapse of the enemy's resistance on Z Day must be borne in mind.

2. In the event of our attaining the objective of the first days operations, quickly and without much opposition, the next steps to be taken require consideration.

3. Two main points must always be kept in view, namely:-

    (a) The objective, when gained, must at once be consolidated strongly.

    (b) Preparations must at once be made for the continuance of the offensive against the next objective.

4. As the attack on the first day's objective progresses and the situation becomes known, Divisions will be informed by Corps H.Q. of the hour at which the final barrage will be lifted to enable patrols to go forward, and the line to which it will be lifted.

    From the same hour III Corps barrage will be kept North of the road running past the North edge of MAMETZ WOOD.

    XIII Corps barrage will not be further West than a North and South line through the Western edge of CATERPILLAR WOOD.

5. If it is found possible to push forward these patrols, they should be directed -

    <u>7th Division</u> - Both through MAMETZ WOOD and round the Eastern side thereof, towards the German 2nd Line at S 14 d 4214.

    <u>21st Division</u> - through MAMETZ WOOD towards the German 2nd Line at S 14 Central.

    These Patrols will be required to send back information -

    (i) To what degree is passable by Infantry.

    (ii) Whether the German 2nd Line is held in strength or not.

6. It must be distinctly understood, and explained to all concerned, that these patrols are intended to reconnoitre and not to fight against any <u>organized</u> resistance. If organized resistance is encountered, the patrols will return and report. They are <u>not</u> to be supported with a view to fighting to gain ground.

7. In similar circumstances, patrols of XIII Corps are in no case being sent North of WILLOW AVENUE STREAM. XIII Corps intend, however, to raid CATERPILLAR WOOD, if circumstances permit.
    Patrols of III Corps are being sent forward to the German second line, North of the road running past the North edge of MAMETZ WOOD, between 2 hrs. 45 and 3 hrs. 30.

8. In the event of the result of the reconnaissances being favourable and orders being given to 7th and 21st Divisions to capture MAMETZ WOOD, the boundary line between the two Divisions xxxxxxxxxx will be X 29 b 56 - junction of tracks X 24 a 6330 - Angle of WOOD at S 23 d 50 - track in S 14 a (inclusive to 21st Division).

    In this eventuality, III Corps may be expected either

    (a) to occupy German 2nd Line from about S 13 b 87 Northwards, or

    (b) occupy with a covering force the general line LOWER WOOD - CONTAL-MAISON VILLA.

- 2 -

8. (Cont.)   XIII Corps will retain the line of their original objective but may be expected to connect with 7th Division at the North Western point of CATERPILLAR WOOD.

9.   Nothing in the above relieve Battalions of consolidating and holding firmly the line allotted.

10.   Rifle and machine gun fire against any airship is absolutely prohibited, unless the airship has revealed its hostile character by dropping bombs.

Instructions will be given when airships are likely to pass in Battalion area, and time. During this time no firing on airships will take place. As it will not always be possible to lay down a route the airship will take, and to act as a warning against fire from our troops, airships will be provided with rockets of various coloured lights. These lights will be changed from time to time. Until further orders, the colour of these lights will be red. Except in the areas and during the periods referred to above, all airships will be regarded as hostile, unless they make the rquired signal.

29/6/1916.

(Sd) H. Broadbent, Lieut. & Adjt.
for Lt-Col. Comdg. 10th (S) Bn. York & Lanc. Regt.

APPENDIX No. 2 to OPERATION ORDERS, dated 23/6/1916.

The following distinguishing badges will be worn in the attack. All ranks must be acquainted with their meaning.

(1) Wire Cutters — a white band 2" wide on the right forearm.

(2) Bombers (who are not on the badged establishment) — a white grenade 2½" in length on the right sleeve, just below the shoulder.

(3) Medium & Heavy T.M. Personnel. — Yellow brassard, 1" wide round each upper arm.

(4) Infantry Runners — a yellow badge 2" square on each forearm.

(5) Signal personnel — Blue and white brassard.

(6) Div. Cavalry and Cyclist Orderlies — Red arm band on right forearm, with "RUNNER" in white letters.

(7) Artillery F.O.Os. — Green brassard on right arm.

(8) Men detailed to collect documents in enemy trenches, dug-outs, or headquarters. — Yellow arm band on right forearm.

24/6/1916.

(Sd) H. Broadbent, Lieut. & Adjt.
For Lieut-Col. Comdg. 10th Bn. York & Lanc. Regt

SECRET.

AMENDMENT No. 2 to OPERATION ORDERS, dated 23/6/1916.

1. Reference para 22 of above, instead of X 29 b 0.5½ read X 29 c 2.9.

2. Each blocking party will remain in the trenches blocked till communication is established with the left Battalion of 50th Brigade, and permission obtained from O.C. that Battalion to rejoin.

3. Stores referred to in para 25 above will be drawn in VILLE.

(Sd) H. Broadbent, Lieut. & Adjt.
24/6/1916. for Lieut-Col. Comdg. 10th (S) Bn. York & Lanc. Regt.

SECRET.

APPENDIX No. 3 to OPERATION ORDERS, dated 23/6/1916.

The following Officers will be taken into the attack:-

H.Q.
    Lt-Col. J.H. Ridgway.
    Captain J.B.O. Trimble.
    Lieut. H. Broadbent.
    Lieut. H.P. Organ.
    2nd Lt. F.E. Payne.

A. Coy.
    Captain D.C.T. Twentyman.
    2nd Lt. R.J. Kingsford.
    2nd Lt. A.L. Quance.
    2nd Lt. J. Douglas.

B. Coy.
    Major A.J. Willis.
    2nd Lt. W.H. Mein.
    3nd Lt. D.H. Drake.
    2nd Lt. C. Sykes.

C. Coy.
    Captain R.W. Mullins.
    2nd Lt. F.C. Cockburn.
    2nd Lt. R.M. Stainton.
    2nd Lt. F. Ayres.

D. Coy.
    Captain F.B. Baker.
    Lieut. E.G.J. Fairnie.
    2nd Lt. R.M. Wilkinson.
    2nd Lt. D.D. Hawley.

(Sd) H. Broadbent, Lieut. & Adjt.
for Lieut-Col. Comdg. 10th (S) Bn. York & Lanc. Regt.

24/6/1916.

SECRET.

AMENDMENT No. 3 to OPERATION ORDERS, dated 23/7/1916.

1. In place of para 2 (b) substitute

   10th York & Lancs. Regt. - X 29 b 5.6 (joining 7th Division) along N. edge of BOTTOM WOOD to X 29 a 5065 (if the high ground at X 29 b 5.6 is not occupied by 7th Division when this line is reached, it will be held by 10th York & Lancs. Regt. with bombers pushed down CLIFF Trench) with Advanced Posts on the line X 29 b 5.6 to X 23 d 1.0.

2. Para 3, sub-section II is cancelled, and the following substituted:-

   The dividing line between Battalions to the Second Objective will be X 28 a 5005 - RAILWAY COPSE (inclusive to 10th York & Lancs. Regt) Railway to the point where it enters BOTTOM WOOD - X 29 a 5065.

3. Water bottles will be carried down from positions in sandbags. Times will be notified.

4. All approximate casualty reports (numbers only) will be sent in to Battalion Headquarters daily by 11.0 a.m. During any lull in operations, steps should be taken to report actual casualties (Names of Officers, and numbers only of other Ranks). The sooner this report reaches Battalion Headquarters the sooner will reinforcements arrive.

5. No public money is to be taken into action by Officers. Steps should be taken to get rid of any spare cash Companies may have.

6. Officers and Platoon N.C.Os will have Nominal Rolls of the men in their Companies and Platoons. No mention of Unit or formation must be made on these rolls. Rolls will be kept strictly up-to-date.

(Sd) H. Broadbent, Lieut. & Adjt.
24/6/1916.   for Lieut.Col. Comdg. 10th York & Lancaster Regiment.

SECRET.

AMENDMENT No. 4 to OPERATION ORDERS, dated 23/6/1916.

1. Reference para 11, the following addition is made:-

    These parties will carry a yellow flag on a stick to show their position. The 10th W. Yorks blocking party coming up from the South will carry red flags.

    These parties will remain in their positions till FRICOURT is clear and the Brigade's right flank protected.

2. Reference para 10.

    The platoon must reach N.E. corner of wood immediately after No. 5 barrage is lifted (2.25 after zero). The 7th Division barrage on that corner will lift at the same time.

    The 50th Brigade advancing through FRICOURT WOOD will reach the track between strong points Nos 5 and 6, and from there send out patrols to get in touch with this platoon.

3. Para 30 is cancelled.

4. Message as follows "ROGER 11 p.m. (or other time as may be ordered) AAA Acknowledge" will denote time of gas attack.

    "ROGER AAA Acknowledge" will be warning that preparations are being made for gas attack.

25/6/1916.
(Sd) H. Broadbent, Lieut. & Adjt.
for Lieut-Col. Comdg. 10th (S) Bn. York & Lancaster Regt.

SECRET.

AMENDMENT No. 5 to OPERATION ORDERS dated 23/6/1916.

In para 23, for 'corner of RAILWAY COPSE' substitute point X 29 c 3.2.

(Sd) H. Broadbent, Lieut. & Adjt.
26/6/1916. for Lieut-Col. Comdg. 10th (S) Bn. York & Lanc. Regt.

SECRET.

AMENDMENT No. 6 to OPERATION ORDERS dated 23/6/1916.

The Battalion will commence the advance from our trenches one hour after zero, the leading waves together near No. 5 barrage as possible with safety, so as to be ready to advance immediately it lifts at 2.25.

(Sd) H. Broadbent, Lieut. & Adjt.
for Lieut-Col. Comdg. 10th (S) Bn. York & Lancaster Regiment.

28/6/1916.

SECRET.

Reference Battalion Orders, dated 23/6/1916, and Amendments.

The Battalion will march to trenches tonight, following 8th Lincolnshire Regt., via MEAULTE, WILLOW AVENUE into HAPPY VALLEY. Head of Column will follow in rear of 8th Lincolnshire Regt. who pass Starting Point (Fork Roads E 25 d Central) at 8.45 p.m. 7th East Yorkshire Regt. follow immediately in rear of 10th York & Lancaster Regt.

In case of necessity, the S.O.S. Signal by means of rockets will be retained in use, viz. 5 rockets fired as rapidly as possible one after the other. These rockets will be sent to Companies on being recieved at the rate of 5 per Company.

Accidents are occurring due to the safety pin of Mills Grenades falling out. All pins should, therefore, be splayed out.

Compass bearings for advance will be

Our dividing line in our trenches to FRICOURT FARM
82½ - 83 degrees. to left edge of FRICOURT FARM.
Thence to point X 29 b 5059 79 degrees.

30/6/1916. for Lieut-Col. Comdg. 10th Bn. York & Lanc. Regt.

(Sd) H. Broadbent, Lieut. & Adjt.

Copy No 12

SECRET.

OPERATION ORDERS, No 2.

By Lieut-Col. J.H. Ridgway,
Comdg. 10th (S) Bn. York & Lancaster Regt.
25th June 1916.

Reference 1:20,000.

1. The Battalion will march on night of 27th/28th June 1916 to VILLE, via CORBIE, MERICOURT and TREUX, head of column passing Headquarters at 9.30 p.m.

    Order of March: Headquarters, B., C., D., A.

    Billets will be taken over in VILLE vacated by 8th Somersets. Lieut. Organ and billeting party will parade at Battalion Headquarters at 8.30 a.m. on 27th June.

2. The Battalion will move to trenches on night of 28th/29th June 1916, head of column to pass Cross Roads E 26 c 7.1½ at 9.35 p.m.

    Order of March: C., A., D., B., and Headquarters.

    Route as already reconnoitred.

    On reaching HAPPY VALLEY Battalion will close up. The 10th York & Lanc. Regt. will use LINDUM STREET and KING'S AVENUE, A. and B. Coys. using KING'S AVENUE, C and D. Coys. and Headquarters using LINDUM STREET. 2/Lt. Mein will report at bottom of ABERDEEN Avenue about F 1 b 8085 to R.A. Officers of 21st and 34th Divs. when the Battalion is in the Communication Trenches, so that Artillery may open fire again without delay.

    The Battalion must be clear of HAPPY VALLEY by 1.30 a.m.

    Stores etc. will be drawn in VILLE at a time to be notified later.

H Broadbent
Lieut. & Adjt.
for Lieut-Col. Comdg. 10th Bn. York & Lanc. Regt.

25/6/1916.

SECRET.

Copy No 12

Reference Operation Order No. 2, dated 25/6/1916.

Para 1 is cancelled, and the following substituted:-

The Battalion will march on afternoon of 27th to VILLE, via BONNAY, then S.E. to Railway nearly to MERICOURT Station, thence across country to BUIRE, thence to VILLE by Road. This route will be reconnoitred by 2/Lt. Mein.

Head of column to pass Y.M.C.A. Tent at 3.0 p.m.

Order of March: Headquarters, B., C., D., and A. Coys.

Dress: Marching Order.

Billets will be taken over in VILLE. Lieut. Organ and billeting party will parade at Battalion H.Q. at 8.30 a.m. on 27th June.

Cookers and Officers' Mess Cart will march to VILLE via CORBIE, MERICOURT and TREUX, starting at 2.0 p.m.

Remainder of Transport, under Transport Officer, will leave LA NEUVILLE for VILLE at 2.0 p.m. Route as above.

A Broadbent
Lieut. & Adjt.
26/6/1916.   10th Bn. York & Lancaster Regiment.

app III

EXTRACT from 63rd BRIGADE ORDERS, dated 30th July 1916.

353. HONOURS AND AWARDS.

The following N.C.Os. and men have been awarded the MILITARY MEDAL:-

10th York & Lancaster Regiment.

No. 19259 Sergt. WILLIAM HATTERSLEY.

On July 1st, when all the Officers of his Company had been hit, this N.C.O. took charge of the Company, rallied and re-organized it and led it forward to LONELY SUPPORT TRENCH.
A few days previous to this he went over the parapet and brought in his Company Commander who had been wounded while examining the wire in front of our line.

No. 16495 Corpl. OWEN HOWSON.

For great gallantry in the field and for the splendid way in which he conducted a bombing attack on the enemy's trenches on July 1st 1916. He and one other man together destroyed an enemy's barricade.

No. 16018 Private AMOS JOY.

This man was a Battalion Runner. He was constantly on the move between Battalion H.Q. and the different Companies. He carried several messages under very heavy fire, and worked himself to a standstill.

No. 15680 Private HARRY JONES.

Devotion to duty and splendid work in bombing the enemy's trenches. At a critical moment he got out of the trench and advanced towards the enemy bombing them from outside their own trench. This action greatly helped to turn the scale in our favour.

-:-:-:-:-:-:-:-:-:-:-:-

EXTRACT from 63rd BRIGADE ORDERS, dates 3rd AUGUST 1916.

262. HONOURS AND AWARDS. Reference 37th D.R.O. 1611.

The following HONOURS and AWARDS have been awarded in connection with the Operations July 1st - 3rd 1916.

10th York & Lancaster Regiment.

No. 4509 Private FRED FOX. Distinguished Conduct Medal.

Stretcher bearer - For devotion to duty and showing absolute disregard for shell fire. He assisted in carrying down a wounded Officer which took several hours to do, and on nearing the Aid Post the whole party was buried by a shell. Private FOX extricated himself and dug out the remainder of the party and the Officer, and when any shell came over he threw himself over the Officer to protect him as much as possible. This man worked himself to a standstill.

-:-:-:-:-:-:-:-:-:-:-:-

CONFIDENTIAL.

10th (Service) Battalion
YORK and LANCASTER Regiment.

WAR DIARY.

JULY, 1916.

ELEVENTH VOLUME.

Army Form C. 2118.

WAR DIARY
10th (Service) Battalion York & Lancaster Regt.
INTELLIGENCE SUMMARY   JULY 1916.

Instructions regarding War Diaries and Intelligence Summaries are contained in F.S. Regs., Part II. and the Staff Manual respectively. Title Pages will be prepared in manuscript.

(Erase heading not required.)

Place	Date	Hour	Summary of Events and Information	Remarks and references to Appendices
VILLE. TRENCHES.	30/6/16 July 1st.	9-0 p.m.	Battalion proceeded from billets in VILLE to ASSEMBLY TRENCHES in DIVNL. SECTOR N.E. of BECORDEL and just W. of FRICOURT. Reference 10th York and Lancs. Operation Orders dated 23/6/16. Z-day. Attack was commenced at 7.30 a.m. by 4th Middlesex Regt. and 8th Somerset L.I. on 21 DIV. Sector. At 8.30 a.m. 10th York and Lancs. and 8th Lincoln Regt. advanced from Assembly trenches and passed through 4th Middlesex Regt. and 8th Somerset L.I. respectively, coming under very heavy machine gun fire from FRICOURT and FRICOURT WOOD. After very hard fighting (in which heavy casualties occurred) the Battalion consolidated in LOZENGE ALLEY and later in DART LANE. Battalion remained in this position till about 2-0pm. third day when it moved up to SUNKEN ROAD, and took up Support Position in DINGLE TRENCH, with H.Q. in SUNKEN ROAD.	App. I App. II App. III App. IV
DERNANCOURT. VAUX-EN-AMIENS TALMAS.	2nd. 3rd. 4th. 8th.	4-0 am. 10-0 am.	Battalion was relieved by one Company 12th Manchester Regt. and proceeded to DERNANCOURT. Entrained for AILLY-SUR-SOMME, where Battalion detrained and marched to VAUX-EN-AMIENS, occupying billets. Battalion proceeded by route march to TALMAS, 63rd Bde. being transferred to 34th Division. Letter issued from Major General Commanding 21 Div. to G.O.C. 63rd Brigade.	App. V
MONDICOURT TRENCHES	9th. 11th. night 13/14th 14th.		Battalion proceeded by route march to MONDICOURT, occupying billets. Battalion proceeded by route to trenches via GRINCOURT-HUMBERCAMP-POMMIER-BIENVILLERS - and occupied trenches 43 - 86 inclusive, relieving 4th and 5th Leicesters (46th Div). 8th Somerset L.I. on our right - and 18th N.F. on our left. Gas emitted from our trenches, raid taking place on our left. Battalion relieved in above mentioned trenches by 5th Leicesters - and proceeded by route to HUMBERCAMP, being billeted night in huts at that place.	App. VI App. VII
HUMBERCAMP				App. VIII
SARS-LES-BOIS. BAILLEUL-AUX-CORNAILLE. ESTRÉE-CAUCHIE	15th. 16th. 17th. 20th.		Battalion proceeded by route march to SARS-LES-BOIS, occupying billets. Battalion proceeded by route march to BAILLEUL-AUX-CORNAILLE, occupying billets. Battalion proceeded by route march to ESTRÉE-CAUCHIE, occupying billets. Battalion inspected by Divisional Commander.	App. IX App. X
TRENCHES.	25th. 28th. night 31st. 1st Aug.		Battalion proceeded to trenches, BERTHONVAL II Sector, Left Sub-Section, relieving 6th Bn. London Regt. Draft of 159 Other Ranks arrived from No. 34 Infantry Base Depot 2/Lt. D.A. HALL joined from 11th (Reserve) Battn. Battalion relieved by 8th Lincolns in above trenches and proceeded to Brigade Reserve, 3 Companies bivouacing in BOIS DES ALLEUX, 1 Company and H.Q. in billets at CAMBLAIN L'ABBE.	App. XI App. XIII App. XII

2449 Wt. W14957/M90 750,000 1/16 J.B.C. & A. Forms/C.2118/12.

LIST of APPENDICES.

I. Battalion Operation Orders, dated 23/6/1916 and additions thereto.

II. Report on Operations July 1st/3rd 1916.

III. List of Honours and Awards of DISTINGUISHED CONDUCT MEDAL and MILITARY MEDAL, in connection with Operations July 1st/3rd 1916.

IV. Casualties incurred in Fighting July 1st/3rd 1916.

V. Letter received by G.O.C. 63rd Brigade from Major-General Commanding 21st Division.

VI. Operation Orders, dated 12/7/1916, for Minor Operation, while Battalion was in trenches near BIENVILLERS.

VII. Operation Orders, dated 14/7/1916, relief in trenches by 5th Leicesters.

VIII. Operation Orders, dated 14/7/1916, move from HUMBERCAMP to SARS-LES-BOIS.

IX. Operation Orders, dated 15/7/1916, move from SARS-LES-BOIS to BAILLEUL-AUX-CORNAILLE.

X. Operation Orders, dated 18/7/1916, move from BAILLEUL-AUX-CORNAILLE to ESTREE-CAUCHIE.

XI. Operation Orders, dated 25/7/1916, move from ESTREE-CAUCHIE to Trenches.

XII. Operation Orders, dated 30/7/1916, move from Trenches to BOIS DES ALLEUX and CAMBLAIN L'ABBE.

XIII. List of CASUALTIES - SICK WASTAGE - REINFORCEMENTS during month.

Lieut-Col.
Comdg. 10th (Service) Bn. York & Lancaster Regt.

app II

10th (Ser) Battn. York & Lancaster Regt.

OPERATIONS
July 1st 1916 -- July 4th 1916.

The Battalion advanced through 4th Middlesex Regt, who were in German front line, and came under heavy machine gun fire from FRICOURT and FRICOURT WOOD. The leading waves got some distance in advance of PART LANE, when they were held up by machine gun fire from FRICOURT WOOD. At the same time three large parties of Germans attempted to bomb their way up all the trenches South of PART LANE. Also at the same time the Battalion Bombers were having a hard struggle with a large bombing party in LONELY TRENCH. They had three barricades in this, which we destroyed. We then placed a barricade at North end of LONELY TRENCH near junction of LOZENGE ALLEY. A party of D. Company with stragglers from other Units were sent into ARROW LANE to protect that flank, with the assistance of one gun of Machine Gun Corps. This party came under heavy fire from the South, the enemy making several strong attempts to bomb up EMPRESS SUPPORT and the remains of EMPRESS TRENCH. The remainder of Battalion were then in LOZENGE ALLEY with 8th Lincolns and parties of other Units. This we were consolidating. About 5.0 p.m. I re-organized the Battalion to take them to PART LANE, which I consolidated. I had also a holding party of Bombers at corner of PART LANE, EMPRESS SUPPORT and LONELY LANE. I had also a party in ARROW LANE and the Communication trenches between PART LANE and ARROW LANE; with this party were about 30 men of 10th Yorkshire Regiment. The Battalion remained in this position till about 2.0 p.m. on the second day, during which time the Battalion was working very hard in passing up S.A.A., Bombs, etc. to 62nd Brigade, who were calling for supplies very urgently. This work went on continuously till about 2.0 p.m. when I was ordered to move up and join 62nd Brigade. I took Battalion up SUNKEN ROAD and put them in DINGLE TRENCH from D 31 Central to about junction of DINGLE TRENCH and PATCH ALLEY, with my headquarters in SUNKEN ROAD at South end of ROUND WOOD.

- 2 -

Whilst here we were under a shell fire from … heavy enemy guns. We remained here till relieved by one Company of ...th Manchester Regt at about 4... a.m. on morning of 4th. The blocking party ordered to follow immediately in rear of 4th Middlesex Regt did not reach their objective, as all the men were knocked out with the exception of about six men, the Officer being wounded just after getting over the parapet. I also collected what spare bombers I had and sent this up to 63rd Brigade, who were calling for more men. The party protecting our right collected a fair number of prisoners from the dug-outs in LAST LANE, EMPRESS SUPPORT and various small communication trenches.

One Officer and a small party of men actually reached the hedge running on outside of FRICOURT FARM, but were compelled to fall back owing to a large bombing party coming down LOZENGE ALLEY from FRICOURT FARM.

Lieut-Colonel.

5th July 16. Comdg. 10th (S) Bn. York & Lancaster Regiment.

Appendix No. IV (a).

CASUALTIES incurred during Fighting JULY 1st/3rd 1916.

OFFICERS.

KILLED - 7.

Rank and Name.	Date.
Captain D.C.T. TWENTYMAN.	1st July 1916.
Captain R.W. MULLINS.	1st July 1916.
Lieutenant H.P. ORGAN.	1st July 1916.
2nd Lieut. R.J. KINGSFORD.	1st July 1916.
2nd Lieut. C. SYKES.	1st July 1916.
2nd Lieut. R.M. STAINTON.	1st July 1916.
2nd Lieut. C.H. GODWIN.	1st July 1916.

WOUNDED - 6.

Rank and Name.	Date.
Major A.J. WILLIS.	1st July 1916.
Captain F.B. BAKER.	1st July 1916.
Lieutenant W.H. MEIN.	1st July 1916.
2nd Lieut. E.C. COCKBURN.	1st July 1916.
2nd Lieut. D.H. DRAKE.	1st July 1916.
2nd Lieut. F. MORTON SMITH.	1st July 1916.

10th (S) Bn. York & Lancaster Regiment.

List of Casualties incurred during Fighting, 1/7/16 - 3/7/16.

Killed in Action, 1/7/16 - 3/7/16.

No. 16770	Pte.	Atkinson,	W.	No. 23134	Pte.	Hooks,	G.W.
No. 14390	:	Jones,	W.	No. 16480	:	Roberts,	A.
No. 21459	:	Smith,	C.H.	No. 24235	:	Jackson,	A.
No. 17750	Cpl.	Brookes,	T.	No. 15981	L/C.	Barlow,	A.
No. 21492	L/S.	Baines,	C.	No. 17735	:	Parker,	R.
No. 21441	Pte.	Barker,	L.	No. 19681	Pte.	Horan,	M.
No. 19361	:	Kerraine,	M.	No. 16748	:	Maher,	T.
No. 19723	:	Wyeth,	B.	No. 19738	:	Cook,	J.
No. 21526	:	Franklin,	T.	No. 18796	:	Howden,	J.F.
No. 17150	:	Leach,	J.	No. 17737	:	Lewin,	A.E.
No. 21475	:	South,	G.	No. 21383	:	Fenton,	E.
No. 19684	:	Jones,	W.R.	No. 23333	:	Thrickett,	H.

Died of Wounds.

Regtl.No.	Rank and Name.		Date.
No. 20882	L/C.	Passmore, E.J.	5/7/1916.
No. 22848	Pte.	Dunn, A.	2/7/1916.
No. 23257	:	Gray, E.	5/7/1916.
No. 22074	:	Holmes, C.A.	2/7/1916.
No. 21482	:	Wilson, H.D.	5/7/1916.
No. 21447	:	South, W.T.	3/7/1916.
No. 23163	:	Owen, G.	3/7/1916.
No. 24305	:	Cole, F.	3/7/1916.
No. 22703	:	Smith, L.W.	6/7/1916.
No. 13648	:	Chevons, Jno.	2/7/1916.

Wounded - reported to England.

Regtl. No.	Rank and Name.		Date of Evacuation to England.	Remarks.
No. 2074	Pte.	Cliffe, J.	4/7/1916.	
No. 15772	Cpl.	Smith, H.	3/7/1916.	
No. 15773	L/S.	Swindall, S.	7/7/1916.	
No. 13560	Cpl.	Wragg, W.	8/7/1916.	
No. 10637	:	McManus, J.	4/7/1916.	
No. 17312	L/C.	Crawshaw, L.	7/7/1916.	
No. 15833	:	Chappell, J.	8/7/1916.	
No. 22684	:	Hancock, H.	4/7/1916.	
No. 7750	:	King, S.J.	3/7/1916.	
No. 9779	:	Marshall, W.	4/7/1916.	
No. 3737	:	Taylor, W.H.	4/7/1916.	
No. 18122	Pte.	Trout, W.T.	4/7/1916.	
No. 19680	:	Bellfield, G.W.	7/7/1916.	
No. 19605	:	Charnock, L.	4/7/1916.	
No. 22880	:	Allott, A.	3/7/1916.	
No. 21505	:	Bingham, H.	3/7/1916.	
No. 17815	:	Brown, J.	3/7/1916.	
No. 11856	:	Brown, L.	6/7/1916.	
No. 21646	:	Bunting, G.H.	12/7/1916.	
No. 21777	:	Chappell, G.A.	3/7/1916.	
No. 17914	:	Disley, J.	3/7/1916.	
No. 15980	:	Griffiths, G.H.	5/7/1916.	
No. 22866	:	James, J.	6/7/1916.	
No. 17393	:	Newett, R.	4/7/1916.	

Regtl. No.	Rank and Name.	Date of Evacuation to England.	Remarks.
No. 21398	Pte. Pickersgill, F.	6/7/1916.	
No. 8578	: Rhodes, J.A.	4/7/1916.	
No. 4172	: Russell, C.	5/7/1916.	
No. 14769	: Turner, W.	7/7/1916.	
No. 18388	CSM. Woods, F.	3/7/1916.	
No. 14422	Sgt. Smith, A.	5/7/1916.	
No. 9323	Cpl. Marshall, H.	3/7/1916.	
No. 14335	Pte. Armsby, J.	9/7/1916.	
No. 23251	: Arnull, F.S.	2/7/1916.	
No. 19241	: Jones, J.E.	7/7/1916.	
No. 15765	: Parker, W.J.	7/7/1916.	
No. 17821	: Ballinger, H.	5/7/1916.	
No. 14461	: Bentley, W.P.	7/7/1916.	
No. 13747	: Butler, J.R.	3/7/1916.	
No. 21199	: Broadby, J.	3/7/1916.	
No. 3120	: Coney, P.	7/7/1916.	
No. 13555	: Davis, F.	3/7/1916.	
No. 4002	: Ellis, J.	3/7/1916.	
No. 11497	: Ellis, F.	4/7/1916.	
No. 15223	: Harris, A.	5/7/1916.	
No. 14081	: Hirst, W.	5/7/1916.	
No. 11472	: Hendley, T.	3/7/1916.	
No. 21849	: Athron, C.	3/7/1916.	
No. 17543	: Kitchen, E.	5/7/1916.	
No. 2846	: Marsh, B.	4/7/1916.	
No. 14917	: Mathewson, G.T.	5/7/1916.	
No. 18371	: Percival, A.	8/7/1916.	
No. 3300	: Parkin, J.W.	3/7/1916.	
No. 19253	: Rylance, J.	3/7/1916.	
No. 19641	: Rigby, J.	13/7/1916.	
No. 3147	: Sumner, G.	4/7/1916.	
No. 19794	: Stones, G.	18/7/1916.	
No. 13759	: Senior, C.	8/7/1916.	
No. 23001	: Stancey, M.	6/7/1916.	
No. 17781	: Tyler, H.	3/7/1916.	
No. 3008	: Wordsworth, C.	7/7/1916.	
No. 18210	: Wild, A.	5/7/1916.	
No. 16526	Sgt. Duncan, T.A.	17/7/1916.	
No. 17549	Cpl. Sykes, N.	3/7/1916.	
No. 21220	L/S. Thackray, F.	9/7/1916.	
No. 20904	L/C. Dickens, L.	5/7/1916.	
No. 18892	: Glennon, T.	3/7/1916.	
No. 9191	: Page, C.A.	3/7/1916.	
No. 20404	: Shepperd, J.	3/7/1916.	
No. 21592	: Ussher, A.E.	3/7/1916.	
No. 23197	: Walker, J.	3/7/1916.	
No. 15875	: Walters, B.	3/7/1916.	
No. 19241	Pte. Jones, J.E.	7/9/1916.	
No. 14771	: Bailey, J.	4/7/1916.	
No. 13876	: Bisby, H.	4/7/1916.	
No. 19798	: Bostock, A.	5/7/1916.	
No. 17385	: Burrell, W.	5/7/1916.	
No. 15587	: Dewsnap, J.	3/7/1916.	
No. 17489	: Dillon, M.	3/7/1916.	
No. 13842	: Doyle, E.	3/7/1916.	
No. 19799	: Frost, R.	3/7/1916.	
No. 19678	: Greenwood, W.J.	17/7/1916.	
No. 7833	: Goose, V.	8/7/1916.	
No. 21484	: Haywood, G.W.	4/7/1916.	
No. 21295	: Heenan, W.	4/7/1916.	
No. 19801	: Holland, J.	4/7/1916.	
No. 16742	: Ibbotson, M.	3/7/1916.	
No. 11075	: Kaye, J.	12/7/1916.	
No. 1689	: Kitching, W.J.	4/7/1916.	
No. 16744	: Leaf, J.W.	3/7/1916.	
No. 19686	: Litchfield, P.	3/7/1916.	

--- 3 ---

Regtl. No.	Rank	and	Name.	Date of Evacuation to England.	Remarks.
No. 23243	Pte.		Lockwood, W.I.	5/7/1916.	
No. 21608	:		Wear, F.	3/7/1916.	
No. 15724	:		Manley, H.	3/7/1916.	
No. 20540	:		Nicholson, W.H.	6/7/1916.	
No. 8872	:		Nuckley, G.	3/7/1916.	
No. 2537	:		Petty, J.	12/7/1916.	
No. 21550	:		Pike, H.	3/7/1916.	
No. 20600	:		Puffett, A.J.	3/7/1916.	
No. 19702	:		Ripley, J.A.	4/7/1916.	
No. 23255	:		Sperring, A.V.	5/7/1916.	
No. 16762	:		Shea, T.	4/8/1916.	
No. 19755	:		Schofield, S.	3/7/1916.	
No. 23266	:		Vernum, C.	3/7/1916.	
No. 24495	:		Wheatcroft, G.	5/7/1916.	
No. 15870	:		Wright, J.	5/7/1916.	
No. 21300	:		Wileman, J.T.	9/7/1916.	
No. 21291	:		Wood, W.	3/7/1916.	
No. 4709	Sgt.		Shipman, E.	6/7/1916.	
No. 19758	Cpl.		Hirst, F.	7/7/1916.	
No. 17726	:		Wilkinson, S.	6/7/1916.	
No. 15722	L/C.		Woolley, J.	3/7/1916.	
No. 19725	Pte.		Acklam, J.	3/7/1916.	
No. 2955	:		Bamford, J.	3/7/1916.	
No. 17896	:		Birch, M.	3/7/1916.	
No. 15822	:		Brown, J.	4/7/1916.	
No. 15673	:		Chance, J.W.	5/7/1916.	
No. 15677	:		Comer, J.	5/7/1916.	
19815	:		Flecknoe, R.	9/7/1916.	
No. 18485	:		Fields, A.	6/7/1916.	
No. 19749	:		Gabriel, J.	4/7/1916.	
No. 16069	:		Gill, G.	3/7/1916.	
No. 18747	:		Gregory, H.	5/7/1916.	
No. 18434	:		Gleeson, J.	4/7/1916.	
No. 22783	:		Higgins, T.P.	5/7/1916.	
No. 19246	:		Lyons, J.	13/7/1916.	
No. 19769	:		Moore, B.	5/7/1916.	
No. 19823	:		Moran, W.	6/7/1916.	
No. 21620	:		McVeigh, S.	7/7/1916.	
No. 17323	:		Pearson, W.	5/7/1916.	
No. 22987	:		Patterson, J.	4/7/1916.	
No. 22993	:		Padgett, G.H.	4/7/1916.	
No. 3050	:		Richards, H.	6/7/1916.	
No. 19781	:		Smyth, J.L.	7/7/1916.	
No. 23180	:		Scargill, G.	4/7/1916.	
No. 2845	:		Shaw, W.	8/7/1916.	
No. 2990	:		Taylor, J.	8/7/1916.	
No. 19830	:		Turton, J.	7/7/1916.	
No. 15692	:		Ward, W.	5/7/1916.	
No. 17604	:		Walker, J.	6/7/1916.	
No. 10729	L/C.		Bower, W.E.	3/7/1916.	
No. 2623	Pte.		Williams, W.	5/7/1916.	
No. 22258	:		Chapman, F.	3/7/1916.	
No. 14818	:		Dyson, H.	5/7/1916.	
No. 21836	:		Heppinstall, F.	7/7/1916.	
No. 22599	:		Hunter, D.	11/7/1916.	
No. 10904	L/C.		Tranter, H.	5/7/1916.	
No. 23237	Pte.		Alcock, W.	4/7/1916.	
No. 16807	L/C.		Waite, F.	6/7/1916.	
No. 17507	Pte.		Brookes, J.J.T.	3/7/1916.	
No. 4509	:		Fox, F.	7/7/1916.	
No. 22762	:		Howson, W.	3/7/1916.	
No. 22175	:		Leach, A.	3/7/1916.	
No. 23094	:		Muscroft, J.	7/7/1916.	
No. 3172	:		Ratcliffe, A.	3/7/1916.	

--- 4 ---

Regtl. No.	Rank and Name.	Date of Evacuation to England.	Remarks.
No. 19701 Pte.	Rees, D.	5/7/1916.	
No. 24007 :	Smith, L.	5/7/1916.	
No. 16800 L/C.	Bamford, N.	9/7/1916.	
No. 22013 Pte.	Greaves, G.	5/7/1916.	
No. 4507 :	Hughes, R.	5/7/1916.	
No. 19831 :	Ware, G.H.	3/7/1916.	
No. 17446 :	Webster, W.H.	5/7/1916.	
No. 21911 :	Cooper, T.	5/7/1916.	
No. 22533 :	Hainsworth, H.	8/7/1916.	
No. 23359 :	Turner, J.	4/7/1916.	
No. 23256 :	Evans, C.H.	3/7/1916.	
No. 16482 L/C.	Shaw, J.	3/7/1916.	
No. 22105 Pte.	Giddons, A.E.	6/7/1916.	
No. 15946 :	Poole, R.G.	4/7/1916.	
No. 23806 :	Monks, J.	3/7/1916.	
No. 24227 :	Jackson, W.E.	5/7/1916.	
No. 10754 :	Milner, C.	3/7/1916.	
No. 23253 :	Frisby, S.	3/7/1916.	
No. 15402 :	Gelder, J.W.	5/7/1916.	
No. 19812 :	Brown, H.	5/7/1916.	
No. 20002 :	Brown, H.	7/7/1916.	
No. 21532 :	Davis, E.	3/7/1916.	
No. 19782 :	Standage, J.	4/7/1916.	
No. 21015 :	Hancock, H.	5/7/1916.	
No. 21443 :	Thompson, A.	2/7/1916.	
No. 14393 :	Dyson, E.	3/7/1916.	

Wounded.

Regtl. No.	Rank and Name.	Information from.
No. 16796 Pte.	Beavon, G.S.	Base.
No. 19262 L/C.	Harrold, G.P.	Company.
No. 19618 :	Price, W.J.	Company.
No. 19624 :	Willman, W.	Company.
No. 13559 :	Wragg, W.	Company.
No. 21649 Pte.	Abbott, H.	Company.
No. 15121 :	Bramhald, G.	64th Field Ambulance.
No. 16794 :	England, J.	64th Field Ambulance.
No. 24498 :	Heathcott, H.	To England - 3/7/1916.
No. 22754 :	Shinwell, A.	64th Field Ambulance.
No. 23713 :	Swift, G.B.	64th Field Ambulance.
No. 13919 :	Thackery, F.	64th Field Ambulance.
No. 8993 Sgt.	Poskitt, G.E.	(Rejoined from Base - 25/7/1916).
No. 13543 L/C.	Butler, F.	Company.
No. 17571 Pte.	Ambler, W.	Company.
No. 16945 :	Acaster, W.	64th Field Ambulance.
No. 15199 :	Knight, S.	Company.
No. 19671 :	Donner, J.W.	Company.
No. 17544 :	Martin, S.	Company.
No. 21943 :	Nicholson, G.W.	Company.
No. 19759 L/C.	Roberts, W.	Company.
No. 22841 Pte.	Roebuck, J.R.	Company.
No. 19795 :	Tighe, L.W.	Company.
No. 11138 :	Ward, C.H.	Company.
No. 19806 Sgt.	Smith, F.	64th Field Ambulance.
No. 18374 Pte.	Silkstone, W.	(Returned to duty - 2/7/1916).
No. 14553 :	Angell, G.	63rd Machine Gun Company.
No. 21339 :	Beachill, A.	Company.
No. 19661 :	Brennan, M.	Company.
No. 19644 :	Cole, C.L.	63rd Machine Gun Company.
No. 21479 :	Graham, E.	Company.
No. 21609 :	Howarth, D.	63rd Machine Gun Company.

--- 5 ---

Regtl. No.	Rank	Name		Information from
No. 23259	Pte.	Law,	E.	Company.
No. 19403	:	McHugh,	J.	Company.
No. 20151	:	Robinson,	F.	Company.
No. 19835	:	Wilson,	A.	Company.
No. 19731	:	Bowman,	T.W.	Company.
No. 17964	:	Holroyd,	A.	64th Field Ambulance.
No. 19759	:	Horne,	A.	64th Field Ambulance.
No. XXXX	:	XXXXXXXX,	X.	
No. 9648	:	Boucher,	H.	Company.
No. 9614	:	Keller,	J.	Company.
No. 22750	:	Gordon,	J.	Company.
No. 3724	:	Simpson,	T.	64th Field Ambulance.
No. 20899	:	Hummell,	C.E.	64th Field Ambulance.
No. 23763	:	Roe,	T.	65th Field Ambulance.
No. 15652	:	Dawson,	J.	64th Field Ambulance.
No. 16747	:	Millar,	J.H.	Company.
No. 21998	:	Noble,	W.	64th Field Ambulance.
No. 21471	:	Steers,	J.T.	Company.
No. 23245	:	Tivnan,	G.	64th Field Ambulance.
No. 22770	:	Booker,	J.	64th Field Ambulance.
No. 4417	L/C.	Dalgarno,	J.	64th Field Ambulance.
No. 3093	:	Wigham,	G.	21st Casualty Clearing Station
No. 16494	Pte.	Holmes,	F.	65th Field Ambulance.
No. 14775	:	Walters,	C.A.	64th Field Ambulance.
No. 15975	:	Darby,	T.	65th Field Ambulance.
No. 22424	:	Park,	H.	65th Field Ambulance.
No.				

Missing.

No. 23206	Pte.	Baldwin,	R.E.
No. 13741	:	Bower,	J.
No. 24044	:	Coates,	W.
No. 13556	:	Fitchett,	W.
No. 23234	:	White,	C.C.
No. 12164	Cpl.	Fletcher,	M.
No. 16562	L/C.	Smith,	J.
No. 14873	Pte.	Houghton,	H.
No. 14914	:	Jenkinson,	G.
No. 13938	:	Leach,	F.
No. 13868	:	Slinger,	A.
No. 3051	:	Smedley,	T.
No. 2976	:	Wedge,	D.
No. 3188	:	Ward,	A.
No. 11406	:	Munn,	H.
No. 23204	L/C.	Sidebottom,	A.
No. 19751	Pte.	Hara,	C.
No. 16737	:	Hayes,	J.H.
No. 3159	:	Heatley,	H.
No. 22532	:	Baldwin,	T.F.
No. 22252	:	Herberts,	E.
No. 24396	:	Parkinson,	W.
No. 22039	:	Turner,	C.B.
No. 21825	:	Simpson,	T.
No. 19768	:	Mason,	J.

Amended Casualties.

Regtl No.	Rank	and	Name.	Previously Reported.	Now Reported.
23206	Pte.	Baldwin,	R.E.	Missing.	Wounded.
11406	:	Munn,	H.	Missing.	Wounded.
23204	L/C.	Sidebottom,	A.	Missing.	Wounded.
3159	Pte.	Heatley,	H.	Missing.	Wounded.
22252	:	Herberts,	E.	Missing.	Wounded.
21835	:	Simpson,	J.T.	Missing.	Wounded.
22039	Pte.	Turner,	C.R.	Missing.	Killed.
12164	Cpl.	Fletcher,	M.	Missing.	Killed.
23259	Pte.	Law,	E.	Wounded.	Killed.
14914	:	Wenkinson,	G.	Missing.	Killed.
19751	:	Gara,	C.	Missing.	Killed.
13938	:	Leach,	F.	Missing.	Killed.
13741	:	Bower,	J.	Missing.	Killed.
13556	:	Fitchett,	W.	Missing.	Killed.
24296	:	Parkinson,	W.	Missing.	Killed.
19664	:	Cole,	C.L.	Wounded.	Killed.
16562	L/C.	Smith,	J.	Missing.	Killed.
13868	Pte.	Slinger,	A.	Missing.	Killed.
3051	:	Smedley,	T.	Missing.	Killed.
21479	:	Graham,	L.	Wounded.	Killed.
3188	:	Ward,	A.	Missing.	Killed.
13543	:	Butler,	W.	Wounded.	Killed.
22352	:	Baldwin,	T.F.	Missing.	Killed.
21330	:	Beachill,	H.	Wounded.	Killed.
19268	L/C.	Harrold,	G.P.	Wounded.	Killed.
21943	Pte.	Nicholson,	G.W.	Wounded.	Killed.
19684	Pte.	Jones,	W.R.	Killed.	Wounded.

The following letter has been received from the G.O.C. 21st Division:-

To/
G.O.C.
63rd Infantry Brigade.

I cannot allow the 63rd Brigade to leave my command without expressing to all ranks my immense admiration for their splendid behaviour during the recent fighting.

No troops in the world could have behaved in a more gallant manner.

I feel sure that the 63rd Brigade will uphold the reputation of the 21st Division in the Division to which they are attached.

Whilst deeply deploring your heavy losses, I feel that these gallant men have willingly given their lives to vindicate the character of the 21st Division.

Hoping that our separation may be of short duration only, I wish you Good Luck.

(sd) DAVID G.M.CAMPBELL, Major-General,
Commanding 21st Divn.

8th July, 1916.

Operation Orders SECRET.

O.C. Companies and Sections.

App VI

On night 12th/13th July gas will be emitted from our trenches, if wind is favourable. A raid will also take place on our left.

Zero time, which is time when gas will be discharged, will be notified later.

At —.30 the front line trenches between 95 and 76 will be evacuated, except for Lewis Gunners, who will all put on their box respirators at not later than —.15. All other men will have their gas helmets rolled on their heads.

It is very probable the enemy will retaliate by bombarding our trenches. Therefore, all except sentries must keep under cover.

Vermorel Sprayers will be kept filled and ready for use, and emptied later if not required.

At +0 our Artillery will fire on enemy front line, and continue till .60, then from +120 to +130. Lewis guns will endeavour to locate enemy's front line machine gun emplacements, and fire bursts of rapid fire.

At +60 light rockets and Strombos Horns may be heard and seen for a little distance on our left. This is only a signal that operations are over.

No patrols will go out tonight. Lewis guns will fire on enemy's gaps to prevent it being repaired. The R.A. have been asked to show where gaps are.

A special code to be used to state whether gas will be liberated or not will be

Probable that gas will be liberated at (hour) - Frankfort... (hour).

Zero Discharge of gas will be at (hour) - Dresden ... (hour).

Discharge of gas postponed - Leipzig.

If gas cannot be liberated, no raid will take place on our left.

On receipt of orders as to time etc., Companies will evacuate all Trenches with exception of Lewis Gunners and a couple of Sentries, one on each flank of their Sector. All other men will be taken to dug-outs on Support Line, or any other dug-outs which are not in Front Line, and remain there till gas and bombardment is over (if there is any), when night positions will be immediately taken up again.

(To be destroyed immediately after operations are finished).

Lieut-Colonel.
12/7/1916. Comdg. 10th (S) Bn. York & Lancaster Regt.

App VII

OPERATION ORDERS

By Lieut-Col. J.H. Ridgway,
Comdg. 10th (S) Bn. York & Lancaster Regt.
14th July 1916.

1. The Battalion will be relieved in trenches tonight.

   4 Companies of 5th Leicester Regiment will take over trenches 73-89 inclusive, as under:-

       73 - 86 from 10th York & Lancaster Regiment.

       87 - 89 from 18th N.F.

   Guides will be provided as follows:-

       D. Coy.   1 Guide for Trenches 73 - 77.
       B. Coy.   1 Guide for Trenches 78 - 84.
       A. Coy.   1 Guide for Trenches 85 - 86.

   To be at barrier on HANNESCAMPS Road E 9 a 7.1 at 7.0 p.m. D. Coy. to lead men up LULU Lane.

   Lewis Gun Guides and one Guide from A. B. and D. Coys. to lead advanced parties to be at same place at 3.0 p.m.

   All guides to have a slip of paper shewing clearly place of rendezvous, Unit to be guided, and destination.

   All kits including Officers Mess Baskets and blankets, to be sent down to Barrier by 7.0 p.m. and handed over to Guard there.

   C. Coy. will carry all dixies etc. down to same place immediately after teas, and will arrange to mount a guard of 1 N.C.O. and 3 men over it. Everything to be out of trenches by 7.0 p.m.

   Companies will hand over all trench stores etc. to incoming Unit, as well as FONQUEVILLERS Map and Trench Maps, and obtain receipts for them.

   The Battalion will be billeted in HUMBERCAMP, the same precaution as before will be observed in marching between BIENVILLERS and POMMIER.

   Billeting party, under 2/Lieut. Samuels, will meet at Barrier at 6.0 p.m. and proceed and take over billets.

   Battalion will march again tomorrow morning.

   Relief complete will be reported at once to Battn. H.Q. by sending the word "VILLE".

                                  (Sd) H. Broadbent, Lieut. & Adjt.
                         10th (S) Bn. York & Lancaster Regiment.

OPERATION ORDERS.

By Lieut-Col. J.H. Ridgway,
Comdg. 10th (S) Bn. York & Lancaster Regiment.
14th July 1916.

App VIII

1. The Brigade will march tomorrow (the 15th inst.) at 8.30 a.m. to HOUYIN, HOUVIGNEUL, SARS-LES-BOIS, and MAGNICOURT SUR CANCHE.

   Starting point: Forked Roads at LA BAZIQUE FARM.

   Order of March: 10th Y. & L. Regt follow 8th S.L.I., head of Battn. to pass Starting Point at 8.43 a.m.

   Hand carts and Lewis Gun Carts will march in rear of Trench Mortar Battery, in above order under Lieut. Elsworth.

   Regtl. Transport will march in rear of Brigade in above order, Head passing starting point at 9.30 a.m.

   Baggage wagons will rendezvous at the Halte on the WARLINGCOURT - SAULTY Road at 9.40 a.m., and there come under orders of O.C. No. 2 Train.

(Sd) H. Broadbent, Lieut. & Adjt.
for Comdg. 10th (S) Battn. York & Lancaster Regiment.

App IX

OPERATION ORDERS.

By Lieut-Colonel Ridgway.
Comdg. 10th Battn. York & Lancaster Rgt.
15th July 1916.

1. The Brigade will march to-morrow at 8.45.a.m. to BAIZIEUL-aux-CORNVILLE(?), CHELLERS and VILLEM-TR.IN.

   There will be two routes.

   Route A. for brigade less 10th York & Lancaster Regt.

   Route B. (For 10th York & Lanc'r only) MAIZIEUL- PENIN-TINGUY.

   Starting point for 10th York & Lancr: Church, CARS-LES-BOIS. Time 8.30.a.m.

   Hand and Lewis Gun carts, 1st Line Transport, water carts, cookers and mess carts, and baggage wagons will march with the Battalion. Orders will be given afterwards dinner en route.

   The Battalion will halt at fork roads immediately S. of TINQUES until orders for billeting are received.

   Reveille: 6.00.a.m.

   Breakfast: 6.30.a.m.

   Wagons including Mess cart, must be packed by 7.00.a.m.

(sgd) H. Broadbent. Lieut. & Adjt.
10th (S) Battn. York & Lancaster Regiment.

app X

OPERATION ORDERS.

By Lt-Colonel J.H. Ridgway,
Comdg. 10th Battn. York & Lanc. Rg
10th July 1916.

1. The Brigade will march today, starting point fork roads N. of R. in CHELERS.

Units will pass starting point in following order at 9.30.a.m. 8th Lincolns, 10th York & Lancs.

1st Line Transport will march under Brigade Transport Officer, transport of 8th Lincolns and 10th York & Lancs. to pass Cross Roads VILLER BRULIN at 10.30.a.m.

Baggage wagons will march with 1st Line Transport.

Battalion will parade at 8.0.a.m.

Order of march: Headquarters, C.A.B.D. D Coy will join Battalion at 7.35.a.m. at Battalion Headquarters.

Kits to be packed by 7.30.a.m. at Q.M. Stores.

Lewis Guns will be packed in handcarts and will march with first line transport.

(sgd) H. Broadbent, Lieut. & Adjt.
10th (Ser) Battn. York & Lancaster Regt.

OPERATION ORDERS.

By Lieut-Colonel. J.H. Ridgway,
Comdg. 10th (S) Bn. York & Lancaster Regiment.
25th July 1916.

The Brigade will relieve 140th Inf. Bde. in Trenches on night 25th/26th July 1916. The 10th York & Lancaster Regt. will relieve 6th LONDON Regiment (left front line).

Battalion will parade at 7.30 p.m. (marching order with steel helmets) in following order. C. B. A. and D., and march via MAISNIL BOUCHIE, CHATEAU de la HAIE, VILLERS au BOIS, to junction of BOYAU 123 and WORTLEY Avenue, where guides will be met at 11.15 p.m. From VILLERS au BOIS, 200 yards interval will be kept between half Companies.

Lewis Gunners, Bombers, Signallers, Snipers, Regtl Sgt-Major, and one N.C.O. per Company will parade at 1.0 p.m., and march by same route to VILLERS AU BOIS; the senior Officer present will pick up guides there at 3.0 p.m. to lead them into trenches. Parties to be marched with 200 yards interval, Lewis Gunners by sections at 100 yards intervals.

Transport Officer will arrange one wagon for Lewis Guns which will be taken to VILLERS AU BOIS, and there unloaded and guns carried. This party will take their tea rations with them, and borrow, if possible, dixies from 6th LONDON Regiment for that meal.

Rations and Mess Cart will follow Battalion, and on arrival at VILLERS AU BOIS will be met by a guide, and taken to dumping ground at CABARET ROUGE. D. Company will proceed with this Transport and carry rations etc. from there to Battalion H.Q.

Officers valises will be handed over to Quartermaster's Stores by 6.0 p.m. tonight for storage.

Companies will report relief complete by sending the word BERTHONVAL.

Water is obtained in the trenches from tanks in ZOUAVE VALLEY.

D. Company will find ration parties and carrying parties daily for taking food up to front line.

Telephones will not be used for messages of any kind between Battalion Headquarters and front line, except S.O.S. and R.A. Tests. Instruments should be tested every ¼ of an hour day and night to see if they are in working order.

(Sd) H. Broadbent, Lieut. & Adjt.
10th (S) Bn. York & Lancaster Regiment.

OPERATION ORDERS

App XII

By Lieut-Colonel J.H. Ridgway,
Comdg. 10th (S) Bn. York & Lancaster Regiment.
30th July 1916.

The Battalion will be relieved in the trenches on night of 31st July/1st August by LAWYER, and take over billets in CAMBLAIN l'ABBE. Time of Relief to be notified later.

Reserve Company will arrange to carry all dixies, baskets etc. to CABARET ROUGE Ration Dump immediately after teas. They will leave a guard over them of 1 N.C.O. and six men. The whole of the stores to be there by 8-30 p.m.

Lewis Gunners will take their guns etc. to the same place as soon as relieved. M.O's panniers will be carried to same spot by stretcher bearers.

Transport Officer will arrange for transport to be there at 10.0 p.m. to remove everything.

Stretchers will accompany Companies and not be placed on Maltese Cart.

Quartermaster will arrange to take over billets in CAMBLAIN L'ABBE from EXCISE, and detail guides to meet Companies coming into village.

Companies will hand over all trench stores and obtain receipts for same.

An interval of 200 yards will be kept between half Companies on getting out of trench, till reaching CHATEAU d'ACQ when they will close up.

Quartermaster's Stores will move under arrangements to be made between the two Quartermasters concerned.

Companies are placed at disposal of O.C. Companies on Tuesday for cleaning up, and washing feet and socks. This latter is most important. There are a great many men going sick at present with sore feet. This is caused by men not taking their socks off and washing them whenever they get a chance, or even turning them inside out makes a tremendous difference. The men should be instructed to do this at every possible opportunity.

In future all Companies and sections will have a foot inspection immediately on the conclusion of a march, or on coming out of trenches on the morning afterwards.

It is hoped to make arrangements whilst in billets to wash socks Regimentally, but this in no way prevents men from washing their own.

Officers' horses will be at the place they were sent back from when coming into the trenches, at 11.0 p.m.

Companies and Sections will report relief complete on passing Battalion Headquarters, and also "all in" on arrival in billets.

The new draft will parade for medical inspection on Tuesday at a time to be notified later.

(Sd) H. Broadbent, Lieut. & Adjt.
10th (S) Bn. York & Lancaster Regiment.

Appendix No.

10th (Service) Battn. York & Lancaster Regiment.

CASUALTIES incurred during the month of JULY 1916.

Date.	Rank and Name.	Nature of Casualty.
July 1st – 3rd.	(See Appendix No. (a).)	
July 11th.	9221 L/Cpl. Cooke, W.H.	Wounded.
	2336 Pte. Swallow, H.	Wounded.
	15140 : Burgin, H.	Wounded.
July 12th.	22423 Pte. Fairweather, A.	Wounded.
	19857 Sgt. Strickland, G.B.	Wounded.
	3184 Pte. Godson, J.	Wounded.
	13778 : Lunn, W.	Wounded.
	11546 : Shelton, A.	Wounded.
	11226 Cpl. Forman, A.	Wounded.
July 26th.	16965 Pte. Batchelor, D.	Wounded.
July 27th.	4221 : Jennison, H.	Wounded (To duty).

SICK WASTAGE.

Officers 1.   Other Ranks.

   (2/Lt. R.A. SMITH).
                                To Field Ambulance.   37.
                                From Field Ambulance. 10.

                                Total Wastage.   27.

REINFORCEMENTS arriving during the month of JULY 1916.

Officers.

   2nd Lieut. D.A. HALL joined on 28th July 1916,
         from 11th (Reserve) Battn. York & Lancaster Regt.

Other Ranks.

   159 Other Ranks arrived on 25th July 1916,
         from No. 34 Infantry Base Depot.

Addition to Orders for Relief.

The Battalion will not be relieved till after midnight on night 31st July/1st August.

The Battalion will not move out of ZOUAVE VALLEY till the whole of 8th Lincoln Regiment is clear of Communication Trenches.

A. B. and D. Companies (under Major Trimble) will take over Camp at present occupied by 8th S.L.I. in BOIS des ALLEUX. These Companies will find nightly a working party of 300 men for work under 152 Field Coy. R.E. on light Railway.

One Officer per Company will reconnoitre the route to the Camp tomorrow before dusk.

Headquarters and C. Company will take over billets in CAMBLAIN L'ABBE vacated by 8th S.L.I.

30/7/1916.

(Sd) H. Broadbent, Lieut. & Adjt.
10th (S) Bn. York & Lancaster Regiment.

www.ingramcontent.com/pod-product-compliance
Lightning Source LLC
Chambersburg PA
CBHW081551160426
43191CB00011B/1901